Praise for

BEYOND THE WALL OF RESISTANCE

“Rick Maurer provides sage advice for dealing with change during these unprecedented and challenging business conditions. This engaging read offers managers and coaches an incredibly useful and timely resource in support of individual, team, company, and shareholder success. If you are dealing with change, you need to read this book!”

Cherie Woodbury
Sr. Vice President, Compliance & Enterprise
Risk Management, Learning & Awareness
Wells Fargo

“Leading change in an organization can be very difficult. The insights and guidance Rick shares in this book have proven to be extremely helpful in understanding and dealing with the predictable challenges that leaders encounter. His approach works!”

Mike Joyce
Sr. Vice President, Operations & Program Management
Lockheed Martin

“I was delighted to see this new version of *Beyond the Wall of Resistance*. It is well researched and credible while written in a user-friendly manner that makes it easy to read and explain to others.”

Kim Davenport
Director of Human Resources
Nissan Americas

"I am happy to recommend this book. It gives a welcome order to dealing with the irrational nature of our organizational lives and does a great job of providing simple stories to make powerful points."

Peter Block
Author, *Community: The Structure of Belonging*, and coauthor, *The Abundant Community: Awakening the Power of Families and Neighborhoods*

"A solid appreciation of resistance, backed with lively, concrete examples from ancient Rome to contemporary Washington. Rick Maurer merges theory and practice so seamlessly I could identify my own experience every step of the way. I highly recommend."*

Marvin Weisbord
Author, *Productive Workplaces Revisited*

"A unique achievement! Resistance to change is treated with the respect it deserves—and Rick Maurer reveals the great power and leverage that come from embracing resistance. A welcome and important contribution to our understanding of the process of renewal."*

Jim Kouzes
Coauthor, *The Leadership Challenge*

"Rick Maurer's approach to managing change through involvement is unique, special, and worthy of any manager's consideration."*

Ron Zemke (1942–2004)
Former Senior Editor at *Training Magazine*, author, and a pioneer in helping organizations learn about customer service

*Praise for the first edition

“Maurer's book is a significant departure from other books on leading change. He tells it like it is. Here's why you fail—and here's what you need to do if you want your pet projects to succeed.”

Cynthia Miller
President
The E Group

“With references ranging from Machiavelli to Woody Allen, Maurer provides an in-depth exploration of the underlying reasons for resistance to change and offers ways to remedy its counterproductive forces. A valuable guide for anyone in business today, from the newly hired business school graduate to the CEO with 40 years of experience.” *

Joe Lane
Former President
IBM Credit Corporation

“Clearly written and action oriented—ideal for anyone with a role in managing a business. Shows how to transform resistance into a positive force—and build strong, long-lasting relationships at the same time. I learned a lot that I can use in my own life.” *

Jerome L. Dodson
President
The Parnassus Fund

“A most relevant topic. All of us experience change or are responsible for implementing change. The book's focus on embracing resistance to better understand its true source is very helpful as are the antidotes and insights from those who have wrestled with change.” *

Bob Druckenmiller
CEO (retired)
Porter Novelli

Also by Rick Maurer

Why Don't You Want What I Want?
Feedback Toolkit
Caught in the Middle
Change Without Migraines Formula

Why 70% of All Changes *STILL* Fail—
and What You Can Do About It

BEYOND THE WALL OF RESISTANCE

REVISED EDITION

RICK MAURER

Austin, Texas

BEYOND THE WALL OF RESISTANCE

Why 70% of All Changes STILL Fail—and What You Can Do About It

Printed in the United States of America

Bard Press
5272 McCormick Mtn. Dr.
Austin, Texas 78734
(512) 266-2112, fax (512) 266-2749
ray@bardpress.com
www.bardpress.com

ORDERING INFORMATION
To order additional copies, contact your local bookstore or email info@bardpress.com.
Quantity discounts are available.

ISBN 13-digit 978-1-885167-72-9, 10-digit 1-885167-72-5 Paperback

Library of Congress Cataloging-in-Publication Data

Maurer, Rick.
Beyond the wall of resistance : why 70% of all changes still fail—and what you can do about it / Rick Maurer.—Rev. ed.
p. cm.
Includes bibliographical references and index.
ISBN 978-1-885167-72-9 (alk. paper)
1. Organizational change—Management. 2. Strategic planning. I. Title.
HD58.8.M3323 2010
658.4'06—dc22 2010015683

The author may be contacted at:

Rick Maurer
(703) 525-7074
rick@rickmaurer.com
www.rickmaurer.com

CREDITS

First Edition
Executive editor: Leslie Stephen
Copyediting: Jeff Morris
Proofreading: Deborah Costenbader, Leslie Coplin
Jacket design: Archetype, Inc.
Text design/production: Archetype, Inc.
Index: Linda Webster

Revised Edition
Managing Editor: Sherry Sprague
Substantive Editor: Leslie Stephen
Copyeditor/Production Editor: Deborah Costenbader
Proofreading: Deborah Costenbader, Luke Torn
Jacket Design: Original revised by Hespenheide Design
Text design/production: Hespenheide Design
Index: Kay Banning

First Edition Hardcover
First printing, January 1996
Second printing, March 1996
Third printing, November 1998
Fourth printing, January 2003
Fifth printing, September 2003
Sixth printing, January 2006

Revised Edition Paperback
First printing, May 2010
Second printing, November 2010
Third printing, May 2013

Dedicated to the memory of my sister,
Laraine, who faced massive change in her life
with grace, courage, and good humor

Table of Contents

1

Why Most Changes Fail

Progress is impossible without change, and those who cannot change their minds cannot change anything.

—George Bernard Shaw
Playwright and Essayist

When I wrote *Beyond the Wall of Resistance* in 1995 about 70 percent of all major changes in organizations failed. According to recent studies the failure rate is still around 70 percent.[1]

Those are sobering statistics.

Since the early '90s there has been a veritable flood of articles and books on how to lead and manage change. I just did an Amazon search on "change management" and came up with 1,318 hits. Over the past fifteen years, most of the large consulting firms created change management practices. Boutique firms were created just to address the challenges of change.

And it is hard to imagine a manager in any organization who has not taken part in some change management training or been given a copy of one of the books on leading change.

That's a lot of information. You'd think we'd be pretty good at making change work by now, but we're not.

So, what is going on?

There is a dilemma. I advise executives on how to lead change. And I find that most know what it takes to plan and lead big projects well. But something gets in the way of turning all of that knowledge into action. Jeffrey Pfeffer and Robert Sutton coined the term "the knowing-doing gap"[2] to describe the large gap between what leaders know and what they actually do on the job.

This is a costly gap.

And things may be getting worse. CEOs say that there is a growing disparity between expecting change and being able to manage it.[3]

Groups that must work together to plan and implement major new initiatives often are located on different continents and are many time zones away from each other. It's harder to lead change today.

With each failed project cynicism builds, making the next project an even harder sell. And each failure means missed opportunities and false starts, with time and limited resources going into trying to manage resistance and indifference. Many organizations cannot afford the luxury of so many failures.

FOUR OF THE BIGGEST MISTAKES LEADERS MAKE

Mistake 1: Assume that understanding equals support and commitment

It is common to introduce change by making a PowerPoint presentation to a large group.

Leaders may schedule time for Q&A, but the questions they get from their audiences tend to be very polite. After all, who wants to tell the boss they don't think this is a good idea? People learn to limit their comments to questions about timelines and budgets. They know those are safe questions. Any reservations or fears go underground and only get spoken about in hallways and carpools.

Since these leaders get so many questions, they may believe that people are interested and ready to work to make this change a success. But the real issues that can kill or damage this project never get on the leaders' screens.

I conducted a study a few years ago and was surprised to learn that the failure to make a compelling case for change was the biggest reason why major new initiatives failed or went off track.

> **TOOLKIT** For the results of this study, visit www.askaboutchange.com and search for **change study results**.

Making a compelling case for change seems to be the biggest thing you can do to build support and commitment for a new initiative, and yet, it is the most overlooked task in the life of many changes.

Mistake 2: Underestimate the potential power of employee (and management) engagement

Many changes in organizations get inflicted on people. Managers and staff are told that a crisis is at hand (or a great opportunity that must be seized immediately or it will disappear). They are told what the organization will do to meet this threat or opportunity. When it will start. Goals and benchmarks. And what's expected of them.

There's hardly a place for anyone to influence any part of the change, from the idea itself to developing plans.

This does work on occasion, but at great cost. The Gallup organization has done extensive research into employee engagement. Here is what they say: "In average organizations, the ratio of engaged to actively disengaged employees is 1.5:1. In world-class organizations, the ratio of engaged to actively disengaged employees is near 8:1. . . . Actively disengaged employees erode an organization's bottom line while breaking the spirits of colleagues in the process. Within the U.S. workforce, Gallup estimates this cost to be more than $300 billion in lost productivity alone."[4]

Organizations give lip service to engagement, but few know what it takes to get the 8:1 ratio that world-class organizations achieve.

Mistake 3: Fail to appreciate the power of fear

Fear of change is deeply personal. The thought of a big change can evoke pictures of relocations or downsizing. People worry that they may be fired. They worry about their families and their careers.

Personal fear trumps the organization's need to change. When fears are triggered, humans' ability to take in information goes down. In other words, people can't hear what we're talking about even if they try. Fear does that to people.

Some organizations trot out research that suggests that a certain percentage of people are early adopters of new things and others are late adopters. They announce this as if there is no way to influence the number of people who get excited about helping a change be successful.

Or leaders apply the stages of death and dying to organizational change. They assume that people will go into denial, get angry, start to bargain, slip into depression, and then accept the change. All the leader has to do is wait for people to get done feeling bad. (By the way, there seems to be precious little to indicate that these stages of grief even fit most people when it is an actual death we're talking about.)

This notion makes a deadly assumption that all changes are good, the leaders know best, and that once employees realize their cheese has moved, all will be right with the world. This view of employees is paternalistic, condescending, and arrogant. These leaders might as well wear t-shirts that read Trust Me, I Know Best—Now Get Back to Work.

Mistake 4: Fail to acknowledge how even a slight lack of trust and confidence in leaders can kill an otherwise fine idea

Trust can make or break a change. But sadly, many who lead change seem to ignore this critically important ingredient. They seem to believe that a good idea will win the day. It won't.

If people don't trust us, why would they follow us? The answer is that most of them won't. On the other hand, if they trust us they usually give us the benefit of the doubt. If we make a mistake, people tend to understand that we are only human, after all. But if trust is low, they listen intently for any word or phrase that could signal that we are about to take them on a dangerous ride.

THERE IS GOOD NEWS

You may have found yourself nodding (privately, of course, so no one else could see you) as you read through that list of big mistakes. If that's so, don't feel bad. You've got lots of company. The good news is: you can avoid those mistakes without a lot of additional cost or effort. And you'll be reaching for the aspirin bottle far less often.

Even though most changes fail, we can learn from those who consistently do change well.

I take the subtitle of this book seriously: *Why 70% of All Changes* Still *Fail—and What You Can Do About It.*

In the first part of this book, I will give you a way to look at change that may be quite different from how you've looked at it in the past. You will see yourself in these pages. At times you may shudder with the recognition of, "Oh, that's me he's talking about," and at other times see why something you did was so wildly successful. You can learn from your mistakes and successes if you keep an open mind.

The second part of the book covers ways to plan and implement change. I will give you opportunities to look at your own leadership practices. Do you and your organization have hidden beliefs that actually block your ability to change? Does your mindset or intention contribute to the success of change, or does it get in the way? How effectively do you engage employees? And finally, what's the gap between what you know and what you do—and how can you bridge that gap?

In the final section, I will cover a range of ways you can apply what you are learning. Think of chapter 10 as a recipe book, offering ideas for working with your team, sizing up outside consultants, and other ways to expand the reach of what you have learned. Chapter 11 shows how to continually deepen your ability to lead change. As you read chapters 2 through 9, I think you will find things you can apply today with a reasonable degree of competence. To develop mastery, leading change is no different than being able to perform a Beethoven sonata or play on center court at Wimbledon. It takes work.

Oh, and those four big mistakes? You'll begin to learn ways to avoid those common blunders in the very next chapter.

Let's get started.

2

The Stages of a Successful Change and What Disrupts It

You philosophers are lucky men. You write on paper and paper is patient. Unfortunately, empress that I am, I write on the susceptible skins of living beings.

—Catherine the Great

Managers at Ajax Paper (a fictitious name), knowing they had to improve quality and productivity in order to survive, decided to initiate an improvement process that relied on high worker involvement. The unions rebelled and closed the facility for six months.

Twenty miles away, a competitor, Beta Products, faced a similar challenge but took a radically different approach. Corporate headquarters would agree to fund capital improvements only if plant management and the six unions would agree to cooperate with each other.

Ajax failed to anticipate the importance of support and the power of resistance. Given their history, there was no reason to believe that the unions would accept a unilateral decision that affected their members in such dramatic ways. Senior management at Beta knew better. They understood that unless they got agreement from all, the chance of success was small.

In this chapter, I cover the Cycle of Change.[1] It describes how the need for change begins to take shape, and how energy begins to build so that we take action which leads to successful completion of the change. I think you'll find the cycle to be a good resource as you think about how you want to approach the next change you lead. You'll also recognize what can happen when you are at one point on this cycle and the people who must support you are somewhere else. I'll use the Ajax/Beta case as we walk through the Cycle of Change.

THE CYCLE OF CHANGE

If we understand that change often follows this cycle, it is easier to predict what's needed at any point in the life of a project. Once we know where we are in the cycle, we begin to see options. Ajax Paper failed to grasp the natural movement of the cycle, whereas Beta embraced it.

The Cycle of Change can help us see

- there is a natural order in the life of a change
- what disrupts that natural movement
- that nothing lasts forever
- the potential consequences of various strategies

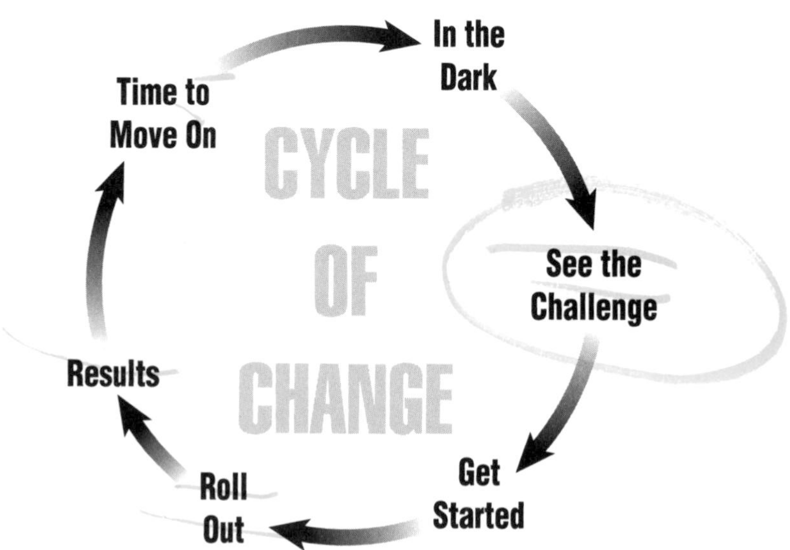

This chart is adapted with permission from the Cycle of Experience developed at the Gestalt Institute of Cleveland.

By understanding the Cycle of Change, you'll begin to see what options make the most sense for leading a change from beginning to end.

In the Dark

There is very little information about the need for change as the cycle begins. But as bits of information come to our awareness, we begin to see a picture emerge. Perhaps this is information that had been in front of us all along, but something happens that jolts us into seeing the implications of the data. Or perhaps, new information comes in—sales figures, your competitor's flashy new product that is getting a lot of attention, a new threat faces the security of your country, or changing demographics in your community that will require new and different services. How you get this information is inconsequential. What is important is that you move from darkness to light.

In the case of the paper plants, there may have been some reports of quality problems and machines needing too much maintenance attention. When senior management in both companies realized there was a problem, most of their respective staffs were in the dark and unaware of the problem.

See the Challenge

This is an "aha" moment when someone recognizes that there is a problem or an opportunity that must be addressed now. At Ajax Paper's corporate headquarters, senior executives saw the challenge and immediately moved to action, leaving plant management and workers behind.

At Beta, senior management opened the books so that everyone could see the challenge facing them.

See the Challenge is the most critical stage of the cycle. Once most people who have a stake in the organization's success see the challenge, it becomes possible to begin to get people aligned to move around the cycle together. Organizational consultant Kathie Dannemiller spoke about the shift that occurs when everyone recognizes the importance of a situation.[2] When this shift does occur, people's views of what's real are transformed. The shift is not just intellectual, it is visceral. Stakeholders begin to see the world from others' points of view. The shift is a realization that you are in this together. You see and *feel* the need for action collectively.

This point is the most important point in the life of a change, but sadly, it is also the most overlooked. Chapter 6, "How to Make a Compelling Case for Change," addresses why this occurs and what to do about it.

By the way, 100 percent of the people don't have to see the challenge in order for an organization to act on the need for change. That would be nice, but it's not likely to happen. However, it is important that a critical mass see the challenge before you move forward. The question of who those people are and how many of them need to see the challenge is something that only you can answer.

Get Started

Once we See the Challenge (or opportunity), energy builds—we want to get busy and do something. Ajax's initial action was unilateral: they wanted to Get Started. Senior management saw a problem and dictated a new program. They did not bother to heighten awareness among staff. At Beta, senior leadership decided to try to bring others out of the dark so that they felt the challenge too. They addressed the question, Can management and the six unions find a way to work together to save the plant? These conversations could take place only after most individuals saw just how dire the situation was for the plant. Once that occurred, they could move into typical getting started activities like identifying the goals, making plans, setting benchmarks, and so forth. Had Beta tried to inflict a plan on people who were still In the Dark, they likely would have had the same problems that Ajax faced.

Roll Out

During this stage, the idea is implemented. For example, an announcement is made: On January 2, we are going to go live with the new software.

At Ajax, they announced the plan and tried to roll out the change quickly. They failed. At Beta, management and the six unions signed an agreement that they all would agree to cooperate with each other to develop plans to bring the plant back to health. Without this, Roll Out would have only been empty words.

Roll Out is sometimes confused with victory. On January 2, you go live and assume that's that. Roll Out is nothing more than flipping the switch and saying you've begun. That's an important point in the life of any change, but that's not the end of the work. You need to see the benefit from all this effort.

Results

At the Results stage, the idea becomes part of the way you do business. Ajax never got close to this stage; Beta was working toward it. Once Beta achieves the goals of improved production and quality, the change itself is over and it's now the new status quo that needs to be managed.

If the change were a fairy tale, the Results stage would end with "and they all lived happily ever after." But life moves on.

Time to Move On

Nothing lasts forever. Even the best plans eventually run their course. Beta may find their agreement with the unions strained as they try to introduce new technology or as foreign competition demands severe cost cutting. If that occurs, they need to realize that actions that worked so beautifully this year may need to be revised or discarded as conditions change.

The transition from Results to Time to Move On is important. Often we hang onto an old idea far too long. It's not that the idea is bad; it is simply time for something else.

When I wrote the first edition of *Beyond the Wall of Resistance* in 1995, I included the following story.

> IBM, once the dominant force in the computer industry, faced hard times in the early '90s. Many observers blame this on the company's inability to shift from mainframe to personal computers. According to Mark Stahlman, writing in the *Wall Street Journal,* IBM did respond to the shift in the market but failed to realize that it would take a new way of approaching the work. They failed to leave Results and move again to the beginning of the cycle. "For a while, it looked as if IBM might be back in the lead. Through a unique combination of events, IBM hit upon the correct new idea": building alliances with others that could provide R&D and partnering with distributors instead of selling only through the company sales force. "But IBM sacrificed this lead by suffocating its infant PC unit with a devastating return to old rules—the mainframe rules." By requiring a standardized software design, the company "killed any capacity within IBM to foster independent business models aimed at separate, unique computer industries."[3]

As I write this revised version in early 2010, I know that the story didn't end there. IBM realized that they were missing a huge opportunity. They went into personal computers with gusto and created well-crafted and well-respected products. And then when that seemed like it had run its course given their goals, they sold the PC business to Lenovo. The cycle just keeps moving.

The Cycle of Change ends and you move onto something new and different, or you use the cycle as a spiral with each change building on the last. (This helps you avoid the "flavor of the month" syndrome.) For example, some organizations embraced quality in the 1980s. When they recognized that quality circles and other similar tools had run their course, they didn't abandon quality improvement; they built on the foundation they had already laid. Some moved to Six Sigma, a process for improving quality out to the sixth standard deviation. As that started to get results, they began to realize that they could take more waste out of the system, so they added in lean manufacturing processes. And on it goes.

WHAT DISRUPTS FORWARD MOVEMENT

Dr. Seuss was wrong. Throughout his classic children's book *Green Eggs and Ham*, Sam-I-Am pesters the unnamed main character until he finally relents and agrees to eat green eggs and ham.[4] In real life, however, the Sam-I-Am approach doesn't work so well. It usually increases resistance to your ideas. Unfortunately, many corporate managers look to Sam-I-Am as a role model.

Change disrupts the status quo. As Arthur Jones says, "All organizations are perfectly designed to get the results they get."[5] Any suggestion of a change disrupts the *perfection* of the status quo. Even if things look dysfunctional to you or you see possibilities on the horizon, that doesn't mean that others see things that way. Unless you can make a compelling case that a change is needed, you are going to get resistance at every step along the way. It is highly unlikely that six months into a big project, people would turn to each other and say, "Wow, was I wrong. What would we do without the brilliant leadership of (fill in your name here)? We are so lucky. She saved us once again."

> **TOOLKIT** For a quick overview of systems thinking as it relates to "all organizations perfectly designed . . . ," visit www.askaboutchange.com and search for **systems thinking**.

We need the voice of resistance. As hard as it may seem at the time, resistance to change can be a very good thing. That's because not all ideas are good ideas. You and I will come up with amazingly idiotic ideas from time to time. We need to be open to criticism from others who see things differently. The history of business and nations is filled with examples of bad ideas that could have been stopped if someone had been willing to listen to the naysayers. I am no longer astounded when line employees,

Sometimes we need to hear the resistance in order to know that our plans are doomed to failure. In The March of Folly, *Barbara Tuchman describes many situations in which leaders failed to read obvious warning signs. In 1685, for instance, Louis XIV rescinded the Edict of Nantes that had provided safety for the Protestant Huguenots, thus opening the door to their persecution. The country praised this action. Even at Louis XIV's death, this was cited as one of his most praiseworthy acts. In what may have been the only dissent, the Dauphin, the king's chief advisor, warned the king that revoking the edict might cause mass emigrations and harm commerce. The king didn't listen, but to his credit, he didn't behead his advisor either.*

The results were devastating. Thousands of skilled workers fled the country, depopulating many regions. Other European nations welcomed the Huguenots with open arms and enticing tax incentives. A Protestant coalition against France was strengthened in Europe. In France, the Protestants who remained redoubled their faith, causing an even wider split between them and the Catholic church. The revocation raised questions about investing monarchs with absolute power. (Three generations later the monarchy was overthrown in the French Revolution.) In all the examples Tuchman notes, the warnings were not only clear but repeated. It's our failure to listen over an extended period that gets us into trouble.[6]

supervisors, and middle managers tell me about some change in their organization that barely has even a chance of succeeding. They talk convincingly about the reasons why that is so. And I wonder, why isn't anyone listening to these people?

But I can also see why leaders don't want to hear bad news. Most of us hate resistance. The mere mention of the word unleashes a torrent of negative thoughts—fear, opposition, conflict, hassles, pain, annoyance, anger, suspicion. Because it is viewed so negatively, people want to get past resistance as quickly as possible.

Another reason that people (including us) resist change is that we have a reaction to the mere thought of this change. In other words, we might agree with the idea itself, but our fear is so strong that our actions work against the change. So why is that a good thing? Because resistance is energy that could be used to support the change, but right now it's tied up in reaction against it. Knowing what resistance is allows you to find ways to turn resistance into support. Much more about this in subsequent chapters.

In the words of so many articles on the subject, people want to *overcome* resistance. This view is wrong. It will get you into serious trouble. Attempts to overcome resistance usually make matters worse. Here are just a few examples that I have seen:

- A merger that never quite merged because little was done to listen to the concerns and ideas of those whose lives were going to be changed. The merger was completed on paper, but the new organization never saw a benefit from the new alliance.
- A new product that died even before it was born because the advocates tried to force its development before other departments had agreed to its merit.
- A construction project that went way over budget because the various groups could not find ways to resolve their differences.
- A quality improvement process that was never fully implemented because no one sought the support of the middle managers, who remained cynical about corporate leadership's commitment to the endeavor.
- A large bank that annually spent hundreds of thousands of dollars for strategic plans that were never implemented because no one, except senior management and the consultants, cared about what was inside the handsomely bound tomes.

Just a quick scan of the business press yields more examples. There is no shortage of failures attributable to poorly handled resistance.

Take the case of the Washington, D.C. football stadium. In the summer of 1992, Jack Kent Cooke, the owner of the D.C. football team, and Virginia Governor Douglas Wilder held a surprise press conference. They announced to a stunned audience that they were moving the team from the District of Columbia to Virginia. They showed precisely where the stadium would be located. They explained how the subway system would add a stop to handle game-day traffic. They showed a model of the proposed stadium. They seemed joyous and excited in their presentation. If someone had handed them shovels, they probably would have started digging the foundation.

Almost immediately, resistance began to develop. The people of Alexandria, Virginia, had other plans for the site. The subway authority didn't want to commit precious funds for a stop that would be used only eight times a year. The citizens of the state did not want to float a bond issue to support the project.

Cooke and Wilder reacted like many people in power: they ignored the resistance and forged ahead. Although nothing can be reduced to a single cause, I believe this was a major factor in the failure of their plans. As they pushed their idea, resistance increased in direct proportion to their actions, and within six months the project was dead.[7]

So instead of the arrow moving around the cycle as they had hoped, the arrow turned inward, and that's where resistance resides. The more they pushed their plan, the more the resistance got embedded even deeper.

Examining this case in terms of the cycle, we can see that Cooke and Wilder were far out ahead of the people of Virginia. They were ready to call in bulldozers. They expected, I am sure, that people would get on board and rapidly move around the cycle to join in support of this idea. It didn't happen. The harder Cooke and Wilder pushed, the more opposition they got.

I find it amazing that Cooke and Wilder didn't seem to learn from this experience and went on to try to build the stadium in Bowie, Maryland. That failed as well. The third location in Largo, Maryland, proved to be the charm and the team now plays there. But think of all the development costs that went into trying to get it built in the other locations.

Shortly after the Northern Virginia stadium failure, the Walt Disney Corporation tried to buy land to build a theme park near Manassas National Battlefield located some thirty miles from the proposed site of the football stadium. Disney failed, in large part, because of the resistance tactics people learned fighting the football stadium.

Here's the danger. Once we get an idea in our heads, it takes on a life of its own. By the time we announce our idea to others, we've hired consultants, ordered the books, and cleared calendars for planning meetings. People rightly say, "What?" They don't see the urgency, consequently they see no need for a grand plan. Our brilliant idea could die before it ever gets started.

THE STAGES OF CHANGE

When my phone rings for advice or consulting help, the request most often falls into one of the following stages.

Making a Compelling Case for Change

This is the most important—and the most overlooked—point in the life of a change. It is the point where a critical mass of those who have a stake in your organization's success say, "We've got to do something differently." They feel this need to change in their bellies. Chapter 6, "How to Make a Compelling Case for Change," explores this stage.

Getting Started on the Right Foot

If you've ever looked at an article on project management, it probably covered the important items that occur in this stage. The one addition to that vast body of work on project planning that often gets overlooked is the question of who do you involve and how do you get them engaged? Chapter 7, "How to Get Started on the Right Foot," examines the work to be done during this stage.

Keeping the Change Alive

This is the second most overlooked point in the life of a change. When all of the hoopla has died down, the work of this stage is to make sure details are attended to in order to get the new system working correctly—things like testing, monitoring closely, and getting the bugs out of the system. The point of Keeping the Change Alive is to get results. So this stage occurs in two parts: get the new system up and running (Roll Out), and make sure all this effort turns into real Results. Chapter 8, "How to Keep Change Alive," covers what to do during this stage.

Getting Back on Track

This stage is often avoidable if you do the other three stages well. But sometimes even the best laid plans derail. During this stage you need to find out why things are going wrong so that you can keep the project on schedule, within budget, and meet your intended goals. Chapter 9, "How to Get Back on Track," covers what to do if you find your project getting off course.

Time to Move On

Each stage of the cycle has in it the seeds of its own destruction. For example, Roll Out won't last forever. It will inevitably lead to Results or failure. Results will either lead to renewal or an ending. And on it goes.

I found that this last stage can easily morph into In the Dark quickly, and that's not a bad thing. I don't cover that stage with much depth in this book. For more on what that stage looks like and what to do about it, I urge you to read *Managing Transitions,* by William Bridges. Although his work looks at the full spectrum of the change process, he describes this limbo stage that I call Time to Move On better than anyone else I've seen. He writes, "Before you can begin something new, you have to end what used to be. Before you can learn a new way of doing things, you have to unlearn the old way. Before you can become a different kind of person, you must let go of your old identity. So beginnings depend on endings. The problem is, people don't like endings."[8]

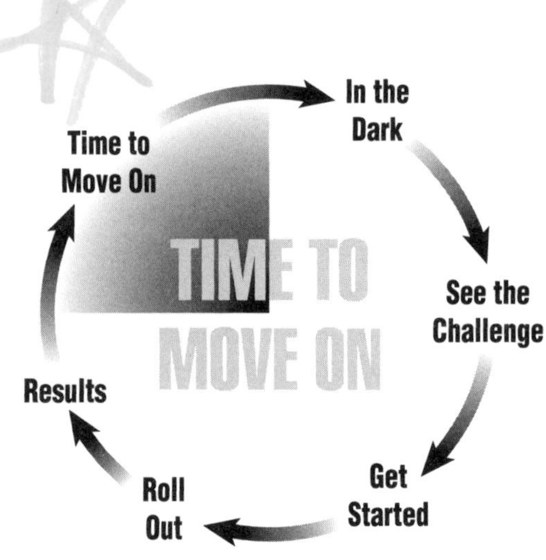

TOOLKIT For a podcast and an article on Gleicher's Change Formula, visit www.askaboutchange.com and search for **change formula**. It is a good resource for explaining the human side of change.

CREATING CONDITIONS FOR CHANGE

I have seen agendas for meetings that look like this one:

Meeting to Plan the New Global Services Process	
Introductions	9:00 to 9:15
Make a Case	9:15 to 10:00
Introduce the Plan	10 A.M. to Noon
Working Lunch	Noon to 1:00
Teams Begin to Develop Plans	1:00 to 5:00
Adjourn	

The agenda looks neat, tidy, and orderly on paper. Unfortunately, people don't see the light, get on board, roll up their sleeves, and get to work according to a predictable timetable.

It just doesn't work that way. People only move from In the Dark to Get Started once they See the Challenge for themselves. That may take moments or months. You can enhance their ability to see the challenge by providing sound information in ways that help them understand the risks (or opportunities) you are facing. But you can't predict when they will see what you see. (Chapter 6 will help you learn how to make a case so that people do see the situation with the same urgency you do.)

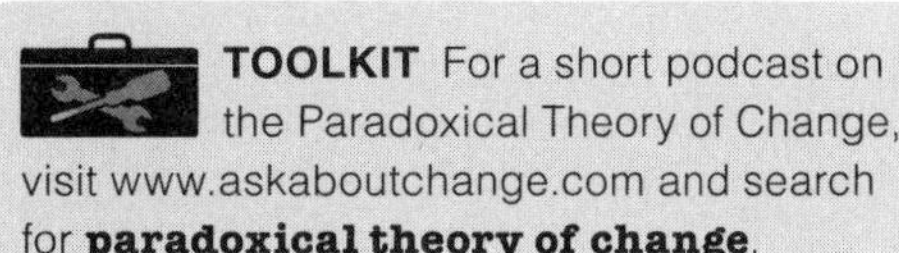

TOOLKIT For a short podcast on the Paradoxical Theory of Change, visit www.askaboutchange.com and search for **paradoxical theory of change**.

Imagine that this agenda is for a meeting that you are running. You make a case, people nod, applaud, and ask appropriate questions. At the stroke of ten they seem to get it. You think, "This meeting is going really well." But, here's the problem. Your audience can fool you and look like they are on board even when they don't know what you're talking about. Admit it, you've learned how to fake it in meetings that you attend as well. You've learned how to act interested. And while you are saying, "Great job, Susan," you're thinking, "What's she smoking this time?"

That insipid show of support will come back to Susan. No one will take on leadership assignments willingly. Arnold Beisser says, ". . . change occurs when one becomes what he is, not when he tries to become what he is not. Change does not take place through a coercive attempt by the individual or by another person to change him, but it does take place if one takes the time and effort to be what he is—to be fully invested in his current positions. By rejecting the role of change agent, we make meaningful and orderly change possible."[9]

He calls this the Paradoxical Theory of Change. The paradox is that you can't make change happen, you can only create the conditions that allow it to occur.

The four chapters in part II cover four stages in depth. Each of those chapters ends with a way to make sure you have done the work needed at that stage before moving on.

BRIDGING THE GAP

All of the chapters through chapter 9 include a Bridging the Gap section. In these sections I offer some suggestions on things you can do today to bridge the gap between knowing how to lead change and actually doing it.

Here is my suggestion with regard to the Cycle of Change. Get the Cycle of Change in your bones. Learn to see the cycle in action. Develop the ability to use it as a tool to plan, monitor, or self-correct situations where two or more people must be in agreement in order for smooth movement from In the Dark through seeing Results to occur.

PART I
KNOWING WHAT TO DO

Rube Goldberg—A comically involved, complicated invention laboriously contrived to perform a simple operation

—Webster's New World Dictionary

As I write this, I am looking at a Rube Goldberg drawing showing how to keep a shop window clean. It involves a man tripping on a banana peel, causing a rake to move upward, propelling a horseshoe onto a rope, and the "invention" is just getting started.

It reminds me a lot of the plans for organizational change I've seen: cobbled together bits and pieces from a variety of sources. Too many steps, too much left to chance, and way too convoluted.

There is a better way. There are many good strategies for planning and implementing change, but you need to know what to look for. The following four chapters will give you a way to begin to look at what it takes to lead change. What to avoid. And what you can do to build your personal capacity to apply what you know.

3

Why People Support You and Why They Resist

The lions might lie down with the lambs, but the lambs won't get much sleep.

—Woody Allen

When a former chairman of the ill-fated Eastern Airlines was once asked what he thought of employee involvement, he replied, "There is no way I'm going to have the monkeys running the zoo."[1] This kind of arrogance makes cooperation extraordinarily difficult, if not impossible. Is it any wonder that Eastern went out of business?

Imagine that you worked for him. How would you react when you heard about the "monkeys running the zoo" comment? Would it inspire you to do better to prove him wrong? (No, I didn't think so.) Would you go to him with your suggestion for improving safety by making a shift in how the company did routine maintenance? (You say you wouldn't! Just what kind of employee are you?) How about when he came up with some grand plan to reorganize the company so Eastern could respond to fierce competition from other airlines? Would you volunteer to help in any way you could? (No? I'm surprised at how negative you are.)

You'll notice that your resistance to the boss wasn't due to some innate character flaw on your part; it was in reaction to his leadership.

This extreme, but all-too-real, example gets at the heart of why people might choose to resist you and the changes you propose. This form of leadership works against employee engagement. Support and resistance are two sides of a single coin. They go together.

Since most changes in organizations require the support of other people, you've got to know where support and resistance come from.

WHAT IS RESISTANCE?

There is hope embedded in resistance, but to find it we must first understand what it is. Although the word is used freely when we speak of change, it is often used imprecisely and incorrectly.

- We use *resistance* to talk about some vague opposition.
- The mere mention of the word may evoke anger at those who have the audacity to resist us.
- We call these people *resistors*, as if resistance were the sole province of a class of people—whom we probably don't like.
- Therefore, it is natural to try to find a way to get rid of it—to overcome resistance.

These views work against our ability to build the support and commitment we need to accomplish any big change (or little change for that matter). Attempts to try to overcome resistance usually just increase opposition. Newton could have been writing about resistance when he said that for every action there is an opposite and equal reaction. With a better understanding of the nature of resistance, you will become more adept at recognizing it in all its many forms and learn how to anticipate and avoid it.

So, what is resistance? It is a force that slows or stops movement. It is a natural and expected part of change. Any system, whether the human body or an organization, resists any change that it believes will be harmful. If you have ever tried to lose weight, you will immediately recognize this dilemma. As you try to lose a few pounds, your metabolism slows to keep you from starving. Your body doesn't know that you are acting on a New Year's resolution. It is simply trying to slow you down so you can conserve energy. Research (but not personal experience) suggests that when you overeat, your metabolism speeds up to keep you at a comfortable *set point* or preferred weight. Your metabolism adjusts to keep your weight steady.

As a company begins a massive reorganization, middle managers may resist because they feel it will harm them. They believe that they might lose their authority or even their jobs. Their set point is the status quo, even though they may actually *see* the need for change. This is not altogether different from standing on scales and resolving to lose those extra pounds. You begin to realize that the mind and the body can work at cross purposes.

As much as you might wish for it, progress without resistance is impossible. People will always have doubts and questions. Even when you are the champion of change, you will still have doubts. Will this really work? Have I given the idea sufficient thought?

Resistance is a natural part of any change. Think of it as protection, energy, and a paradox.

Protection

Resistance protects us from harm. It keeps us from skiing down treacherous double black diamond slopes after our first lesson on the bunny hill. It alerts us that taking that chair lift to Bodycast Mountain is foolhardy and hazardous to our health. In organizations, it keeps us from saying yes to every boneheaded idea that some overzealous manager dreams up. By resisting, we may save ourselves lots of unnecessary work, pain, and migraines.

From the vantage point of the person resisting, caution is absolutely the right course of action. When we are the ones resisting, we see it as a positive force. It keeps us safe. Resistance can be a sign of health, a way to navigate in a complex and rapidly changing world.

Just imagine if you said yes to everything everyone asked of you. When your boss, co-workers, employees, partner, kids, telemarketers call—you say yes. It is resistance to that onslaught of requests and demands that keeps you from being overwhelmed by all those demands.

If we can remember that people resist for good reasons—that they usually aren't out to get us—then we can begin to approach them differently. Keeping this thought in mind may allow us to search for ways to work with others rather than inflicting something on them.

Energy

Resistance is energy. If you have ever faced a room full of people angry at some action you took, you will have no trouble recognizing this unique brand of energy.

The energy of resistance can be a powerful and frightening force. You may be inclined to meet this force with force. Even though you may overpower and win the battle, you will lose the war because you have lost the commitment you so desperately needed. Your goal should be to help redirect this energy. In the martial art of Aikido, the purpose is to find the harmony in conflict. When an opponent punches, the master does not counterpunch but joins the energy of the attacker's force. He might step to the side, lightly take the adversary's arm, and move with him. By blending his movement with his opponent's, he protects himself, and the opponent saves face. The master accomplishes this without kicking, taunting, or sucker punching his adversary.

A Paradox

Resistance is part of any desired change. When you want something new, resistance comes up. As I write this chapter a few days after New Year's, I am staying away from my health club because I know that all the cardio and weight machines will be in use. All the floor space will be covered with brand-new Spandex outfits. I'll wait until February when all this will change. The people who made strong New Year's resolutions to get in shape will realize that they moved to action (Roll Out on the cycle) without thinking through some of the forces that could work against this new goal. Having to get up an hour and a half earlier. And having to go to bed earlier. And having to start eating tofu instead of Bud's Big Heart Attack Burger with bacon and brie. Their New Year's enthusiasm put them out ahead of themselves on the cycle.

It is possible, even likely, that personal and organizational changes put what we *say* we want into conflict with what we may *really* want, say to sleep in and eat Cheetos. This tension between want and resistance has kept psychologists busy for decades.

The paradox is that the desire to get in shape and the desire to eat what you like and sleep until noon are at war with each other. Affirmations—"I look like Brad Pitt," "I am the Angelina of my neighborhood"— might work for a minute in getting you up out of bed. But those silly positive-thinking mantras wear out fast.

I believe the people who do go to the gym regularly are aware of the competing forces at play. Every day when the alarm rings at 5 A.M., they need to decide anew to get up, even though another voice says, "Ah, sweet sleep, just another few minutes."

This same pull between what we say we want and what we really want occurs in organizational change. In later chapters I will discuss ways to bring resistance out into the open. We don't do this for its own sake, but in the belief that when enough attention and respect are paid to it, resistance can turn to support. Full awareness of the desire to sleep for another thirty minutes and the reasons why that is so appealing begin to allow us to see options. This is the Paradoxical Theory of Change at play.

A Dancing Lesson

The transformation from resistance to support can occur if we are willing to be part of the process. As we learn about the reasons why others resist us, we can be influenced. We begin to see the subtle interplay as they resist, we react, they resist anew. We now have a choice: we can keep sparring, or we can dance. If we choose the dance, we move back and forth, one influencing the other, until it becomes difficult to recall who resisted and who initiated. We can influence resistance only if we are willing to be influenced by people resisting us. This means giving up our certainty. It requires suspending disbelief.

> *The human brain is, in large part, a machine for winning arguments, a machine for convincing others that its owner is in the right—and thus a machine for convincing the owner of the same thing. The brain is like a good lawyer: given any set of interests to defend, it sets about convincing the world of their moral and logical worth, regardless of whether they in fact have any of either.*
>
> —Robert Wright
> *The Moral Animal*[2]

The big lesson is that resistance occurs in the relationship between those other people and us. There are no born resistors. People react in response to something we do. They may lean back with fear, concern, and confusion, or they may lean in with excitement, wanting to know more and discovering how they can join this parade. And we, in turn, are leaning in or leaning away in response to the other person. It's movement back and forth. It's a dance with both partners leading and following.

WHY PEOPLE RESIST YOU[3]

There is resistance and there is *resistance.* Although some situations are so deeply embedded in organizations that cooperation seems impossible, most situations are not that intractable. Unfortunately, the idea of resistance is so powerful that it may cloud your judgment, making it difficult to distinguish minor criticism from full-blown animosity. The more you know about why people resist, the more options you have for avoiding it or turning it into support.

There are three reasons why people resist change.

3

LEVEL 1: I DON'T GET IT

Level 1 involves facts, figures, and ideas. It is the world of thinking and rational action. It is the world of presentations, diagrams, and logical arguments. PowerPoint, for instance, is a fine Level 1 tool, but its usefulness is usually limited to Level 1 issues.

Level 1 resistance may come from

- lack of information
- disagreement over the interpretation of the data
- lack of exposure to critical information
- confusion over what it all means

You may believe you can convince others by stating the situation from your own vantage point. A number of years ago I was in the market for a laptop computer. My only resistance to buying was minor: can I get what I need at a reasonable cost? Not knowing a lot about the workings of computers, I tuned out quickly when people launched into talk of bits and bytes. After several exasperating encounters with computer salespeople, I entered a store near my office with some trepidation. I assumed I would hear the same intimidating barrage of technical jargon, but this salesman was different. He asked what I wanted to use the laptop for. It was so simple, but no one had asked me that question before. I told him I needed to do word processing and send email. He seemed surprised. "That's it? That's all you need? Then this is what you want." He showed me a fairly inexpensive machine and assured me it would do what I wanted. No talk of esoteric computer stuff; he limited his remarks to addressing my questions in language I understood. I didn't shop around—I bought that laptop.

The salesman did what so few of us do very well, and that was to listen and speak my language.

Risks at Level 1

Giving people information is the most common way organizations try to deal with resistance. Many make the mistake of thinking that all resistance is Level 1. Just give people more facts and figures and they'll see the light. They hold more meetings and make more PowerPoint presentations when something completely different may be called for. That's where Levels 2 and 3 come into play.

Left unattended, Level 1 resistance can intensify. For example, if you push to Get Started or Roll Out while people are still questioning your sanity, they will dig in even harder.

A common fantasy is that once others see how good the change will be, they will move quickly around the cycle and join in. But you must ask yourself, when was the last time that happened? You must deal with the resistance as soon as you recognize it or else run the risk of allowing it to deepen.

Most people fear dealing with resistance at any level. So even a simple Level 1 challenge like "We don't have enough staff to do that" may make you apoplectic. The slightest opposition may feel like a personal attack. You ascribe evil motives to the person who dared challenge you and respond with an inappropriate knee-jerk reaction (covered in chapter 4). You have now entered the world of Levels 2 and 3.

LEVEL 2: I DON'T LIKE IT

Level 2 resistance is an emotional reaction to the change. Blood pressure rises, adrenaline flows, pulse rate increases. It is based on fear. People are afraid that this change will cause them to lose face, status, control—maybe even their jobs.

Level 2 emotions are not wishy-washy. You can't tell people to "just get over it" and expect them to respond with, "Wow, thanks, I needed that." Level 2 runs deep. When we experience Level 2 ourselves, it can feel as if our very survival is at stake.

Communicating is difficult at this level. When adrenaline shoots through our bodies, we shift into a fight-flight mode (or perhaps we are immobilized like a deer in headlights). Our ability to listen shuts down. No matter how terrific your presentation is, once people hear the word "downsizing," their minds and bodies go elsewhere. This reaction is uncontrollable. They are not choosing to ignore you; it's just that they've got more important things on their minds—like their own survival.

Organizations usually don't encourage people to respond emotionally, so employees limit their questions and comments to polite Level 1 issues like "How much will this cost?" or "What's the timeline?" These questions may make it appear like they are in sync with you, but they are not. They are asking Level 1 questions with a hope that you'll read between the lines and address their Level 2 or Level 3 concerns. And they may not even be aware that they are operating on such a basic emotional level.

The Risk of Level 2

You may try to deal with deeper levels of resistance by using Level 1 strategies, but such superficial approaches cannot reach people's concerns and yearnings. Personal fear and yearning are not in the vocabulary of most business organizations. As you get close to these emotionally charged feelings, your tendency is to run or to blame those who resist—not because they are resisting, but because you cannot imagine engaging them at so deep a level. Meeting people at Level 2 takes courage.

During one meeting I attended, a CEO said that he had just ordered his head of human resources to lay off a number of staff—and that "as soon as he gets that done, I'm going to fire his ass too." I believe his crass insensitivity masked an inability to make human contact with his staff. He had to send an emissary to do his dirty work and then, to isolate himself from the pain, "fire his ass" as well. (Note that he couldn't even dignify the person with a name, only a body part.)

TOOLKIT For a quick podcast introduction to research on Level 2 reactions, visit www.askaboutchange.com and search for **Level 2**.

In contrast, a plant manager was brought in to close down a failing operation. He did it with such transparency about what was going on that people gave him a standing ovation.

He knew that they would be experiencing a lot of deep emotions like loss and fear for their own futures. He didn't sugarcoat or deny reality. He treated people with the respect they deserved.

If you allow yourself to stay removed from the human toll, you cannot build support for your ideas. In the first example above, those remaining in their jobs will undoubtedly fear that the same thing could happen to them.

LEVEL 3: I DON'T LIKE YOU

Maybe they do like you, but they don't trust or have confidence in your leadership. I know that's a hard pill to swallow, but lack of attention to Level 3 is a major reason why resistance flourishes and changes fail.

Your relationship with others who have a stake in the change matters quite a bit. But this is seldom talked about. Books on change often talk about strategies and plans, but most of this advice fails to recognize the fundamental importance of trust in leading change successfully.

In Level 3 resistance, people are not resisting the idea; they may even love the idea. They are resisting *you*. Maybe their history with you makes them wary. Perhaps they are afraid that you won't see things through and this will be another "flavor of the month" scenario. Or that you won't have the courage to make the tough decisions. Or that you'll be rotated to another assignment before this change ever gets rolling. Or that you are nothing but a yes man for the big boss.

Perhaps it's not you, but rather it's that people may resist who you represent. The moment they hear that someone from IT, HR, headquarters, or management is coming to "help," they get skeptical and afraid (Level 2 mixes with Level 3).

Whatever the reasons for Level 3 resistance, you can't afford to ignore it. It can make or break you.

Level 3 concerns don't have to be true in order for them to hinder your ability to get things done. If people believe that you can't be trusted, they'll act on that belief until proven otherwise.

Historic animosity can meet conflicting values and vision. Think about the centuries-old conflicts in the Middle East, Northern Ireland, the Cold War in the decades after World War II, and the pro-life versus pro-choice debate. Progress when animosity is deeply embedded can take decades, even centuries, to turn fierce opposition into any semblance of common concern. But witness some of the strides made in Northern Ireland and South Africa in the past twenty years, and you can see that progress, though difficult, is possible.

The good news for leaders in organizations is that no matter how deeply embedded the animosity is, it's probably not nearly as entrenched as the situations I just named. But, it does take work and an amazing amount of persistence.

Turning Level 3 resistance into support can be extremely difficult. Don't expect a speech or some dramatic event on your part to turn things around. You've got to prove that you are worthy of their trust. That occurs when people believe that you have their best interests at heart. That takes time and skills that many leaders don't possess. The good news is that you can learn how to be more trustworthy.

The Risk at Level 3

Anything can go wrong when you walk into the Level 3 minefield. Trust is so low and the animosity so deep that the slightest misstep can set progress back months or years. It is especially tempting to quit mid-journey and revert to something out of the Attila the Hun playbook. Don't do it. Better not to have attempted anything than to have to use force against the other parties.

Also, it is hard to get good information about what people really think of you. People want you to be in a fog of ignorance. Samuel Goldywn, the famous movie mogul and cofounder of MGM, once said, "I want people to tell me the truth even if it costs them their jobs." If you're the boss, people have a great incentive to lie to you.

THE POSITIVE SIDE OF THE THREE LEVELS

The three levels of resistance play off each other, one influencing the other. A mistake at Level 1 can have an impact on Level 2 fears and Level 3 mistrust. That's why I asked an artist to create the icon you see here. It depicts the vibrant and sometimes messy interplay among the levels.

And actions that begin to build trust—even in a small way—have a positive impact on people's emotional reactions and their ability to hear what you have to say.

These levels are always in flux, sometimes moving in your favor, sometimes not. Effective leaders I consult with are pretty savvy about where things stand with people who they want to influence.

Combining the Positive Side of Levels 1, 2, and 3

In *The Diffusion of Innovations,* Everett Rogers identified five important factors in getting new ideas across to others.

1. **Relative Advantage.** People need to *see* how change is better than the status quo. Information systems departments that set out to build strong computer systems often succeed by showing their companies why an investment today will pay off later.
2. **Compatibility.** People must see the link to the old way of doing things. For many years, the late Felix Grant was the preeminent jazz disc jockey in Washington, D.C. Radio station managers generally thought that jazz was too cerebral or ethnic for broad audiences. Grant realized that most station managers knew very little about music, so he called his show *The Album Sound.* "I dealt with them in the beginning by never using the word 'jazz.' I would play Sinatra, who was very big then, but I would play the hipper things that nobody else was playing . . . and the non-jazz fan for the most part wouldn't really know that it was jazz. He just heard good music, music that wasn't played much anywhere else. And it worked out very well. They sold a lot of spots and the station was happy."[4]
3. **Simplicity.** As excited as you may be by the new idea, you must keep it simple. I believe that one of the reasons why Facebook, Twitter, and other social networking sites have been so successful is that they are easy to use. In the earlier days of the Internet, online communities were cumbersome affairs limited to people with the stamina to find ways to navigate the arcane instructions of those sites.
4. **Easy to Test.** People need a chance to experiment with the new ways: What if I don't like it? What if it doesn't work? Rogers cites a 1943 study that found that all the Iowa farmers who adopted hybrid corn used it first on a trial basis.[5] Widespread adoption would have been much slower without this trial period.
5. **Observability.** It's easier to accept something new after you've seen it in action. Many organizations, before adopting new technology in management systems, send staff on field trips to see

> how others are using it. During these trips, people can "kick tires" and ask tough questions. Rogers describes how people learn to accept innovations. Substitute "major change" for "innovation" and his comments are equally relevant. Although people do pay attention to objective studies or scientific evaluations, most people adopt an innovation only after seeing how it works for other people just like them.

On the other hand, although people are most likely to accept innovations from people who are like them, most new ideas come from people who are different. It is their difference that lets them see things from another vantage point. It would be nice if they were like us in every way except the new idea, but they are usually quite different. "They simply do not talk the same language," writes Rogers. That's why leaders must find common ground with those they hope to influence.

Resistance gets our attention because it is a force working against our projects and sometimes our dreams, but we may take support for granted. I urge you to consider thinking about the three levels throughout the life of a change. When things are working well, stop for a moment and think about why people are interested—even excited—about your project. You can learn a lot from what you are doing right. It is far easier to build on what's working well than trying to correct what's failing, as you will see in part II of this book.

TOOLKIT For a quick podcast introduction to Rogers' pioneering work, visit www.askaboutchange.com and search for **Rogers**.

HOW TO RECOGNIZE RESISTANCE

Archaeological remains show that when Pompeii was buried by the eruption of Mount Vesuvius in A.D. 79, villagers were caught completely by surprise. Presumably no one saw the devastating earthquake of A.D. 62 as a sign that the old volcano was still active; as a result, two thousand people were killed in the eruption.[6] Today, we know the signs of an impending eruption. It is important as well to know the signs of resistance; otherwise, you risk becoming a victim of the blast.

But spotting resistance only lets you know that something is going on. That observation usually doesn't let you know if it is Level 1, Level 2, Level 3, or a combination of the levels at play. (In chapter 9, I'll discuss ways to find out what's behind the resistance you are observing.)

Here's what to look for:

Confusion

Even after you have tried many times to explain the new program, people still ask basic questions: "Why are we doing this?" "Who am I going to report to?" "How much is this going to cost?" "Where did you say you wanted to build that?" Assuming that you *did* explain things clearly, this confusion is one form of resistance.

People are not lying to you. Resistance creates an aural fog that makes it difficult for people (ourselves included) to hear what's being said.

Our own confusion may make it difficult for us to hear others when they are saying things we don't want to hear. And that just adds to the confusion.

Sometimes confusion is simply confusion. At other times, it provides protection from taking in information people don't want to hear.

My Suggestion: Patiently answer their questions for the twentieth time, but realize that something deeper is probably at play. My guess is that it's not safe to ask the burning Level 2 or Level 3 questions. You'll need to find another way to learn what those concerns are.

Immediate Criticism

Even before people hear all the details, often they express their disapproval. Groucho Marx once sang, "Whatever it is—I'm against it." This instantaneous negative reaction to you and your ideas can be maddening. Have you ever worked in an organization where people routinely oppose the slightest change? Even before the idea is fully explained, they begin mounting their criticism. It is as if they have been there before and know exactly what to expect. By the way, this immediate criticism can be delivered softly and with great civility.

When individuals or groups criticize too quickly, it is likely that they have been burned in the past and have developed a shell of resistance. They may feel that if they allow anything through that shell, they will be hurt again.

My Suggestion: Assume that the immediate criticism is masking a Level 2 or Level 3 concern. Instead of being angry at their quick retorts, be grateful that they just gave you a hint that you need to dig deeper.

Denial

People put their heads in the sand and refuse to see that things are different. Often, the more you try to justify, the deeper they embed themselves.

In his PBS series *Healing and the Mind,* Bill Moyers spoke with a cardiologist who refused to admit that he had a serious heart condition. For years he refused even to look at his electrocardiogram. Our wish to not see what's in front of us can be extraordinarily strong—so strong that even a doctor who specializes in the heart won't admit the truth to himself.

Denial can cause the leader to not hear legitimate concerns about the brilliant ideas they have just developed.

Unless someone is consciously trying to manipulate you, deflection is a form of denial. People keep changing the subject. Meetings flit from topic to topic. Just as you start to talk about something of substance, someone brings up another perhaps equally important topic, and all attention shifts to it.

Like all other forms of resistance, deflection is a way people have of protecting themselves. Changing the subject is like raising a shield to stop an incoming arrow.

Deflection can be unconscious and not a strategic choice. Managers in a small manufacturing plant routinely used discussions of their budget as a way of avoiding talking about other issues that affected their work. It was much safer to talk about numbers than about the things they were doing that inhibited each others' productivity.

My Suggestion: Realize that denial and deflection often come from the fact that what you are suggesting is just too scary to look at directly. Avoid going into Level 1 oversell. Try to appreciate that their denial is sending you a message.

Malicious Compliance

People smile and appear to go along with the decision. It is only later, when they drag their feet, that you learn the truth.

The president of a small company was excited about initiating new management procedures. He was an enthusiastic champion, and no one wanted (or dared) burst his bubble. People agreed with him in public. It took months before he realized that managers were doing only the minimum necessary to keep this change alive.

Malicious compliance is often done with full awareness. People usually know that they are trying to trick you into believing that all is well.

As a leader, you employ malicious compliance when you nod in mock agreement during a meeting with the headquarters staff. As you nod like a bobblehead doll, you know that you are doing that just to get them out of your office and back on a plane.

My Suggestion: This is a Level 3 issue. Malicious compliance stems from either a lack of trust in you or who you represent, or a desire to not hurt your feelings. They may like you a lot, but don't want to let you down to your face, so they lie. Once again, be grateful for getting that news, and begin to find out what's behind the "everything is going great, boss" responses.

One way to do this is to ask the following question: "I'm glad to hear things are going so well. How did you solve that problem with the contabulator bearings?" Or, "Great, let me see what you've come up with." You need to listen for substance and not just the words you want to hear.

Sabotage

Outright sabotage is usually easy to spot. People take strong actions that are specifically intended to stop you from proceeding. Software strangely breaks down; a machine malfunctions at an inopportune time; messages don't get delivered. If there is a positive side to sabotage, it is that there is little doubt that someone or some group is strongly opposed to your plans.

Like malicious compliance, sabotage is frequently a conscious act. Think of the French Resistance during World War II.

But people can also sabotage without being aware that they are doing so. Even leaders can sabotage. Think about those times when you "inadvertently" forgot to invite someone to an important meeting or didn't notice him as he tried to get your attention just as you were about to take a vote. Sabotage comes in many forms.

My Suggestion: Take sabotage very seriously. It is risky for people to put their careers on the line by throwing boots into the machinery (which is one possible origin of the term sabotage). You've got to find a way to get the Level 2 and Level 3 issues out in the open.

Easy Agreement

People agree with you without much criticism. On the surface, this might seem ideal. You present your plan, people applaud wildly, so it seems to be time to move ahead.

Although they may sincerely wish to go along, their quick acceptance could spell disaster later, when they realize what the changes mean. They have swallowed your message whole without digesting it, like crazed young lovers who vow eternal devotion after the first date. The difference between easy agreement and malicious compliance is less in the action and more in the intent. People who give easy agreement truly believe the idea has merit. It is only later that they realize the implications of their hasty Las Vegas wedding.

ADC Kentrox, a manufacturer of telecommunications equipment, was so eager to implement ISO 9000 standards that "they almost destroyed their company." They followed the ISO guidelines diligently, without adapting them to their organization, and created a massive bureaucratic nightmare. One senior product manager was ready to resign, believing that this "monstrosity" would kill the company. Knowing that the red tape would add months to projects, managers ignored the company's new 100-page document on ISO standards. According to David Kenney, director of quality, "We had not considered our company's situation: we are a small, market-leading company with 250 employees. We needed flexible, quickly implemented procedures—the opposite of what we had created in our attempt to please ISO's auditors. Armed with these conclusions, we restructured the new-product introduction process to include decentralization of responsibilities and a flexible approach to project management."[7]

My Suggestion: Challenge people. You might say, "I am delighted that you are so excited about the idea. But before we rush ahead, let's discuss the implications of a possible change on budget, staffing, and how we do our work." This conversation causes all of you to chew your food and to consider possible consequences of taking some action. Then if you get agreement, it is more likely to be real support rather than easy agreement.

Silence

You present your idea, the lights come up, and you look out on a corporate Mount Rushmore—chiseled stone faces giving no hint of what they think. Do people agree? Are they too stunned to speak? Are they afraid to talk?

Silence is a difficult form of resistance to address because it gives you so little to work with. And, of course, since silence sometimes does indicate support, it is hard to know what to make of it.

My Suggestion: As a general guideline, never assume that silence means acceptance. In your own desire to get things moving you may be tempted to make that faulty assumption, only to learn later that no one was with you. Better to slow down and find out what's behind the silence.

In-Your-Face Criticism

With no holds barred, these people tell you exactly what's on their minds. They often have a reputation for their impolitic and impolite manner. I remember Joe, who worked for a government agency. His boss hated it when he showed up for meetings. Joe just said it like he saw it. He did not understand the phrase "career limiting move." He just lit into his boss. As hard as it was for my client to listen to this guy, Joe was saying things that no one else had the guts to say. You may not like it, but the Joes of the world can be invaluable.

As a leader, you may be tempted to use an in-your-face approach when you try to get your point across. Sadly it usually builds opposition to you and your ideas. I speak from personal experience. Years ago I conducted a leadership development seminar for government managers. One man in the course criticized everything I said. I could see others roll their eyes when he spoke, so I thought it safe to go on the offensive. I was brilliant; Hawkeye Pierce was never so facile. My retorts were like rapiers. Surely this would shut him up and endear me to the hearts of others.

I was wrong. People sided with him. After all, he was one of their own, and I was the outsider. I spent the next two days digging myself out of the hole that I had dug for myself.

My Suggestion: You may want to dismiss their comments because of their grating and belligerent manner, but that would be a mistake. Unlike the others, these people are telling you the truth as they see it. Often they express what other, milder souls are afraid to say to you. Since others may not respect them, you could be tempted to lash out to make them shudder with your withering sarcasm. Don't. Avoid brilliant comebacks. They just make it unsafe for others to speak.

It is important to keep refining your skills at recognizing resistance. The more skilled you are at seeing the face of resistance in its many forms, the quicker you will be able to address it.

BRIDGING THE GAP

Be able to recognize what prompts the shifts from support to resistance and vice versa. It is easiest to start by watching other people work with each other. It's not only easier, it's more fun. I am writing this in an airport that is a hotbed for tempers flaring as flights get delayed, bags end up on some undiscovered planet, and precious seat assignments go to the "wrong" people.

Awareness is key. In chapter 11, "Moving Toward Mastery," I provide suggestions for ways to learn to work with resistance. But for now, you can learn a lot just by watching.

The next chapter covers knee-jerk reactions. These are the things that can kill otherwise wonderful plans. They are the things we do before we think.

Taking Their Side

An Interview with Peter Block

Peter Block is the author of many important books, including Community: The Structure of Belonging, *and co-author of* The Abundant Community: Awakening the Power of Families and Neighborhoods, *and is a highly regarded organizational consultant. He has a unique ability to state clearly what others wish they had said. I have long admired his thinking on the subject of resistance.*

RM: Peter, how do you handle resistance?

PB: I don't believe that resistance is a problem or something to be overcome, so part of how I handle it is how I think about it. We rarely experience our own resistance—so we don't want somebody to overcome it. All the combative language about resistance only intensifies it: If we overcome it, get around it, reduce it, deal with it—all those verbs indicate that it is a problem to be solved. Resistance is simply a reluctance to choose.

We have just not made up our mind whether to yield and surrender to what's asked of us or to keep on as is. Our inability to choose is an emotional issue usually stuck on questions like: "What's the point? How optimistic am I about the future and what it holds? How vulnerable do I feel at this moment?"

RM: What do you do when you face people who resist you?

PB: I say, "How can I take their side?" They must be acting with good cause, with good reason, so I support the resistance. I support people not making a choice—I can also live with whatever choice they make.

The problem occurs when I have a stake in their actions. Then I need to ask myself, "Why is that a problem? Who am I to say what they ought to be doing? Who is to say that I am the enlightened one?"

RM: How do you support a client's resistance?

PB: I exaggerate. I love the edge. If people are fearful, I reframe their fear in life and death terms. If people are having trouble influencing others, I say, "What if there is no way in the world they will ever go along with you?" Somehow in the extreme people can let go of their caution, their judgment, their ambivalence. I think extreme language dramatizes choice. And I make light of what first seems heavy. I might say, "So, what's the problem? You're going to die anyway. Why don't you just decide what position you want to be in when it happens?"

RM: You've said that you love the phrase, "What you see is what you get." How come?

PB: It makes me responsible for the universe and it puts my life back in my hands. It forces me to question my view of events and gives me an enormous amount of choice over how I experience the world. I like this idea. Someday I hope to experience it.

RM: Any words for those people who think all this is garbage and want to overcome resistance?

PB: I'd say, "Do you want to win or do you want to work things out? Maybe you're reading the wrong book. Maybe you should read *You Are What You Eat.*"

4

The Danger of Knee-Jerk Reactions

Always forgive your enemies—nothing annoys them so much.

—Oscar Wilde

Harry ran a large project for his company. He was bright, arrogant, and wanted to get his way. (You may have met him.) When he felt challenged, his voice changed. His voice got shrill and lost the nuance and music that had been in it just moments before. In the early days of the project, his team didn't know that Harry really didn't want to hear their opinions—he only wanted them to go along with his ideas. But being bright and eager team members, they would try to prove their worth by showing him different ways to look at a problem. That got him angry, and he would begin talking in longer stretches. It almost seemed like he didn't have to breathe. There was seldom a pause long enough for anyone to get a word in. Pretty soon, people got the message. When he speaks, you nod your head, and for God's sake, shut up.

He got compliance from his team (they knew gainful employment when they saw it), but he seldom got the full commitment he was looking for. He created his own resistance and consequently diminished his power to influence others. And he had to take on a lot of extra work to make sure it got done right. His habitual knee-jerk reactions done him in.

When we face resistance to our ideas, most of us have an arsenal of automatic ways we can respond. These defensive reactions are often prompted by fear. In these instances it is our own Level 2 reaction to something the other person or group does that triggers our amygdalae, which then shoot adrenalin into our system. Within a fraction of a second, we respond with a fight, flight, or a stunned reaction. In this state, we are off-balance and unable to work with others with any degree of subtlety or sensitivity. In fact, when we are in this state that Daniel Goleman calls "an amygdala hijack,"[1] we can't even hear emotional nuance. And for a very good reason—we are fighting for our survival, or fleeing, or looking dead-on into the headlights without a clue what to do.

But sometimes we react quickly, and our actions are completely out of context. When Ted Conover went undercover to write about life as a guard at Sing Sing Prison, he was given advice from other guards on how to protect himself. And he learned what it took for a guard to survive in a maximum security prison. He writes, "'Leave it at the gate, you hear time and time again in correction . . . don't bring it home to your family. This was good in theory. In reality, though, I was like my friend who had worked the pumps at a service station. Even after she got home and took a shower, you could still smell the gasoline on her hands. Prison got into your skin, or under it. If you stayed long enough, some of it probably seeped into your soul." He goes onto tell a heartrending story about telling his three-year-old son to not wake up his sister. When the boy disobeyed, Conover ran upstairs and picked him up. "'When I say no, you will listen,' I whispered angrily, and gave him a spank, surprising myself."[2]

Sometimes a knee-jerk reaction is simply our habitual way of working with others. Perhaps we've never seen anyone lead any differently, so that's what we do. Or conditions in the environment cause us to act a certain way. And sometimes that works and sometimes it doesn't.

The consequences of knee-jerk reactions can work against the relationships we so desperately need with other people. In the first example, Harry's strong reaction worked against the possibility of learning anything from his team or creating the type of high-performance that he wanted. Conover found that behaviors that worked well on the job were beginning to be harmful knee-jerks at home. He was responding to stimuli from his child in ways that just weren't appropriate to their relationship.

KNEE-JERK REACTIONS

I have identified eight knee-jerk reactions, but you may have some personal ones to add to the list.

Defensive Use of Power

For many, the way to work with resistance is to immediately try to overcome or overpower it—to meet force with force. The only way to decrease opposition is to squelch those who disagree. This use of power may be subtle: a gentle reminder that lets people know who the boss is or a joke during a meeting just so that no one forgets who conducts their performance reviews. Or it may be blatant: ranting, raving, and striking fear into the hearts of those who dare go against the leader's wishes.

The use of power is not a bad thing if you use it with your eyes open. You understand the consequences of taking a strong assertive stance. And you can adapt as conditions change. But that's not a knee-jerk reaction. The knee-jerk version of using power is anything but that. It is an unconscious reaction to something that hooks us and throws us off-balance. In knee-jerk mode it is hard for us to turn down the volume.

When power is used on people, it drives the arrow down into the center of the Cycle of Change (into resistance) faster than just about any other action. Unbridled power almost guarantees a strong response: it could be a use of force coming back at us or people getting out of our way as fast as they can.

Manipulate Those Who Oppose

Manipulation enjoys a long, rich history. In 1532, Niccolò Machiavelli wrote *The Prince,* a self-help manual for those aspiring to power. His advice on how to acquire and use power included ways to skillfully manipulate others—methods that are as effective today as they were half a millennium ago. We may conveniently fail to tell people the whole story until they have agreed to go along. We meet behind closed doors to determine ways to apply pressure on our opponents.

When we are caught up in this knee-jerk reaction, manipulation seems like the only way to respond. We might think, "How can I con them into going along?"

It is important to distinguish between the trickery described above and a more positive and conscious use of strategy. For example, it makes perfect sense to determine who might be the best person to talk with staff about an upcoming change. Who has credibility? Whom will they listen to? Even though that decision might be made behind closed doors, the intent is to increase communication, not to trick people into complying.

When people learn they've been tricked, your credibility (Level 3) goes down and the memory of that manipulation can have a very long half-life. People will remember and warn others to be wary of you.

Force of Reason

When we use force of reason, it is easy to overwhelm others with facts, figures, and flowcharts. We kill them with data. This is the Sam-I-Am tactic. Giving people information can sometimes be a good way to deal with resistance, but this strategy is too much of a good thing. When we use it, it turns up the volume way too high on Level 1 data.

When we employ force of reason, it's hard to shut up. If they disagree, we figure they must be stupid, so we explain it over and over again.

A manager asked for advice on how to build a bridge between his department and one down the hall—two departments that had long been enemies. Each side spoke badly about the other, and when they had to work together, each entered projects with reluctance and suspicion. People played their cards close to the vest.

My client's plan was to *tell* his counterpart all the reasons why he should want to build this bridge. I said, "Frank, it sounds to me like you want to *Law & Order* them to death—give the jury such a barrage of facts that they can't help but throw up their hands and agree with you." Frank's intent was good; they *should* find ways to work cooperatively. But his courtroom lawyer style left no room for dialogue or for an exploration of why tensions ran so high between the units. In the past when he used this approach, it just made matters worse. But he found that he kept getting triggered by something they would say, and off he would go into force-of-reason land.

People feel insulted when we use force of reason on them. They feel like we are treating them like children. They rarely respond with pleasure and appreciation for our tenacity. They just get angry. At the very least, they simply tune out when we talk. When we open our mouths, their thoughts go elsewhere.

Ignore Resistance

Sometimes we view resistance like gnats at a picnic—a minor nuisance, but nothing to get concerned about. It seems that Cooke and Wilder ignored mounting resistance when they tried to talk people into allowing them to

Since dealing with strong resistance is difficult, we sometimes allow our worst fears to take over. In the classic comedy movie Duck Soup, *Rufus T. Firefly (Groucho Marx), leader of Freedonia, waits for the arrival of the ambassador from the neighboring country of Sylvania. The ambassador's apology, and Firefly's acceptance, would avoid a war that neither side can afford. But as Groucho waits, his thoughts run riot.*

> *I'd be unworthy of the high trust that's been placed in me if I didn't do everything in my power to keep our beloved Freedonia at peace with the world. I'd be only too happy to meet Ambassador Trentino and offer him, on behalf of my country, the right hand of good fellowship. And, I feel sure he will accept this gesture in the spirit with which it is offered. But suppose he doesn't? A fine thing that'll be. I hold out my hand and he refuses to accept it. That'll add a lot to my prestige, won't it? Me, the head of a country, snubbed by a foreign ambassador. Who does he think he is, that he can come here and make a sport out of me in front of all my people? Think of it, I hold out my hand and that hyena refuses to accept it. Why, the cheap, four-flushing swine. He'll never get away with it, I tell you, he'll never get away with it. [Trentino enters ready to make peace.] So, you refuse to shake hands with me, huh? [Groucho slaps him and the war begins.]*[3]

build a new stadium. After all, they were very powerful men, used to getting their way. How could little, poorly funded community groups possibly be a threat to an idea whose time had come?

Sometimes we might ignore resistance simply because we want to believe that no one could seriously question our plans. We fail to see opposition mounting in front of us. The fantasy is, if we just keep moving forward, others will join in.

The problem is that when we are in the emotional throes of this (or any) knee-jerk reaction, we often lack the capacity to see conditions change. Rome burns, and we blame it on global warming but never realize that we were the ones who started the fire.

Play Off Relationships

We use our friendship or common experience as a tool to get others to agree to our plan. They go along, not because it is such a good idea, but because they feel they owe it to us. This strategy often crumbles once people realize that our plan will cost them time or money—or runs counter to plans of their own.

If the change is minor, playing off relationships will probably work fine, but you are not reading this book to learn how to deal with insignificant changes. It is important to find ways to get others deeply interested in your ideas. And that means you need to be willing to learn about and work with Level 2 and Level 3 issues. You can't jolly your way out of Level 2 fear or Level 3 distrust. You must engage others and be willing to be influenced by their ideas as well.

The only not-so-negative thing about playing off relationships is that the insignificance of our actions probably won't offend anybody. But that's hardly a stunning endorsement for this tactic.

Make Deals

Deal making is how the U.S. Congress works: I'll give you this, if you'll give me that. Deal making works fine if all you need is someone's vote. It can also work if resistance is low and the other people don't have a particular preference about the direction we intend to take. It does not work if resistance is high and if we need passion and commitment from people to support and implement the plan.

If we revert to this knee-jerk, we may find that our overtures fall flat. No harm, no foul, but no success either.

Kill the Messenger

When the news is bad, instead of being thankful, we get rid of the people who dare question us. A VP in a privately held company told me that whenever the company hired a new manager, the other junior executives warned him to never criticize an idea of the owner in a meeting. Invariably, some eager young manager, who wanted to prove that he was a worthy addition to the team, would point out a flaw in the boss's assumptions or plans. That eager new manager was never seen again. The manager and his ideas had been dismissed.

If you have someone in your organization who is willing to tell the truth as he or she sees it, or is willing to ask impolitic questions, you may need to curb your desire to figuratively kill that messenger. Remember, that person may have something important to tell you.

The risk of killing the messenger is that by attacking Melissa, everyone in the room—or anyone who reads her texts or tweets—will know about it. Even if others feel Melissa might deserve to be put in her place this time, it won't matter. You will lose. The word will get out that it is dangerous to say anything that might upset you.

Give In Too Soon

We may believe that the resistance is so strong that we give up before we ever know the true level of opposition or whether there might have been a way to arrive at some common understanding. I have seen middle managers so beaten down by the bureaucracy that they give up almost before they begin. They seemed to live under a cloud of pessimism. As soon as the clouds began to darken, they abandoned their plans. They seldom waited to see how strong the storm could be. These people fail to see the context. They can't see when it might be safe to join the conversation.

WHY THE KNEE-JERKS SELDOM WORK

There are a number of reasons why knee-jerk reactions are dangerous and should be avoided.

They Assume That You Are Right and They Are Wrong

The dirty secret is that all these knee-jerk reactions are variations on exactly the same thing. They are built on the assumption that you are right and the other people are wrong. No need to listen. No need to be influenced. All we need to do is to get them to do your bidding. That's quite an arrogant stance.

Imagine when you are on the receiving end of various knee-jerk reactions. How do you react in the moment? What's the longer-term ramification of that exchange? That's what happens when we—without thinking—inflict a knee-jerk on others.

They Increase Resistance

When you give in to knee-jerk reactions, you turn the exchange with that other person into a contest. Whose idea will win?

When people feel they have something to lose, they often fight back. When Cooke and Wilder ignored the opposition, the residents of Northern Virginia formed groups to fight what they saw as a threat to their community.

Many societies value win-lose situations. Every night, television serves up protagonists who win over their opponents. The sports pages tell us in banner headlines who won and who lost. News stories are framed as battles between adversaries, even when the contest seems to be only in the eye of the reporter.[4] This mindset can be so pervasive that we fail to even see that there might be other alternatives.

The problem with a win-lose mindset is that it limits our options when cooperation is called for. I like sports; I don't want baseball to change into some New Age event where no one wins. But in the workplace, an us-versus-them model can be a killer. As our product design "team" tries to get a new product to market, we engage in a "full court press" to get it out the door before accounting can object. Headquarters "drives home" a new initiative. Our "home runs," "slam dunks," "two-minute drills," and "blitzes" make competitors of the people who should be our business partners.

Although we call this *healthy* competition, it is anything but. Assuming that our new idea will face stiff opposition, we begin to view the fight to save our dream as a battle royal. To the victor belong the spoils.

If competition is the only way, then it will be impossible to build alliances with all who have a stake in the outcome. Competition causes us to assume that our interests are at odds with those of other people, even though they may be sitting in the office next to ours.

The Win Might Not Be Worth the Cost

In 279 B.C. the emperor Pyrrhus fought the Romans at Asculum. His army won, but at a tremendous cost in lives. He was said to have declared, "One more such victory and I am lost."[5] Such Pyrrhic victories are common in organizations.

Our desire to win at all costs blinds us to the toll it takes. 20th Century Fox tried a new way of selling movies to television. Instead of selling rights for a fixed fee, they set up bidding wars between the networks. One of the first films offered was *The Poseidon Adventure*. The network executives couldn't stop themselves, even when they realized they had gone over their break-even point. It wasn't that they wanted the film so badly—they just didn't want another network to get it. ABC finally got the rights to show the film a single time for $3.3 million, knowing that they would probably lose over a million dollars![6] That was in 1973; in today's dollars the loss would be the equivalent of almost $5 million.

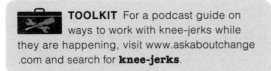

> **TOOLKIT** For a podcast guide on ways to work with knee-jerks while they are happening, visit www.askaboutchange.com and search for **knee-jerks**.

ABC's "win" only cost them money. When competition this intense occurs inside an organization, your win can leave a bitter taste in the mouths of the losers. The Pyrrhic nature of the victory becomes evident when we try to build support for our next change. It is then we realize the cost of winning was too high.

Game theory teaches that in economics, trade, and even war, the unbridled urge to win escalates conflicts, often resulting in stalemates or extremely costly victories. Game theory searches for alternatives to these zero-sum games (games with a winner and a loser—or in this case, two losers) by suggesting that players look for strategies in which both sides can either win or keep losses to a minimum.

WORKING WITH YOUR OWN KNEE-JERK REACTIONS

Among these strategies you may recognize two or three of your personal knee-jerk favorites. Don't feel bad; these are the ways most of us first react when people resist us. We anticipate what others might be thinking, and suddenly we find ourselves using a strategy without thinking about it.

The key is not allowing that internal reaction—that shot of adrenalin—to throw us off balance.

It is also important to consider your personal knee-jerk reactions as well as those your organization typically uses. For example, you often may use force of reason, while the corporation tends to use power without ever thinking about it. Consider how you deal with resistance at both levels, the personal and the organizational. Understanding how you typically respond is the first step in finding better alternatives.

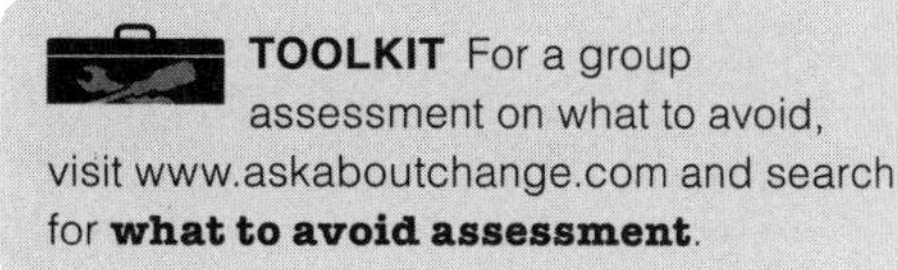
TOOLKIT For a group assessment on what to avoid, visit www.askaboutchange.com and search for **what to avoid assessment**.

BRIDGING THE GAP

Learn what triggers knee-jerks in you, and then begin to notice the early warning signs. Experiment with ways of avoiding these reactions or ways that you might get out of a mess mid-jerk.

Hint: The best early warning signal is your body: it reacts instantly. Muscles tighten. Fists clench. Heart rate increases. These signals are available to us far more readily than our thoughts or feelings about the situation. In the world of knee-jerks, thoughts and awareness of feelings come ages after the body first reacts.

The Unspoken Game

An Interview with Geoffrey Bellman

Geoffrey Bellman is a consultant and author of How to Get Things Done When You're Not in Charge *and co-author of* Extraordinary Groups: How Ordinary Teams Achieve Amazing Results. *I am impressed by his willingness to look inward and his candor in expressing what he finds. Even though he speaks about his unique role as a consultant or change agent, I think you'll find his words speak to all who work inside organizations.*

RM: Where does resistance come from?

GB: It doesn't have to do with what's present here in this system. It has to do with the games we are playing in our lives—what we need to be in our own lives. Change agents have defined ourselves as being different from the systems we work in. We have a great resistance to "getting in bed with them," talking like them, losing our specialness. We are afraid we'll be just like them, that we won't be "special" in the ways that we've defined it. Our supposed specialness springs from a little bit of hierarchical thinking: I'm better, they're worse. Listen to how we talk about the people we work with. At the base of it we're all a bunch of naked human beings. Down underneath it all, in the game we never talk about—the primary game—we're all down there reaching, grasping, clinging, lifting, floating through life. And that's what we have in common—when we take off all the armor—with the organizations we work in. But we seldom acknowledge this. We're all equal in that regard. We all share a resistance to looking into the deeper meaning of what we are doing. We all resist looking deeply into why we are doing what we are doing. And at the same time, we resist letting go of those reasons.

RM: So what can help us begin to understand that unspoken game we are each playing?

GB: Let go of the idea that we are ever going to fully understand it, but always keep trying to understand the unspoken game. We are always going to be discovering more about ourselves, our games. We need to acknowledge that the game goes beyond our ability to make sense of it. It is a fascinating life mystery. I know this sounds impractical, but it is practical as hell. Another point: Whenever I tell clients to "Do this," "Don't do that," I imply that the game is "solvable." It is not. My advice, my techniques, tools, and models are only attempts at fuller understanding; these tools will not give me answers, the complete picture. I need to remind myself of that; I need to remind my clients of that.

RM: Since we so much want to be in control of situations, this sounds very difficult.

GB: Yes. But the tools are just tools, though they do help us find our deeper meaning. But if I can approach the new discoveries about myself with a positive "exploring the mystery" perspective, then new discoveries become new openings. Any personal game becomes much richer than I ever imagined. Richness and frustration seem to go hand in hand, but staying in the searching mode allows me to accept the game as it is.

5

Ignore the Context at Your Peril

We usually only see the things we are looking for, so much so that we sometimes see them where they are not.

—Eric Hoffer

On February 1, 2003, the Shuttle Columbia burned and was destroyed on reentry into the Earth's atmosphere. An independent commission was appointed to examine the cause of the accident and make recommendations. They wrote that they "intended to put this accident into context."[1] The report went on to say, "We considered it unlikely that the accident was a random event; rather it was likely related in some degree to NASA's budgets, history, and program culture, as well as the politics, compromises, and changing priorities of the democratic process. We are convinced that the management practices overseeing the Space Shuttle Program were as much a cause of the accident as the foam that struck the left wing."

If we are looking for one thing—say the technical reasons why an accident occurred—we will limit what we see and risk missing something equally or more important. By forcing ourselves to look more broadly and ask, "What else could it be?" we expand the frame and allow for a broader and even deeper understanding of the problem or problems.

When the world economic crisis hit in 2008, we—the press and the public—looked for who was responsible for this meltdown. We had to have a villain. And there were villains, but by solely focusing on the cheats and crooks, it distracted us from looking at the underlying causes of the crisis. Complexity came later. Context matters.

WHY WE MISS THE CONTEXT

The more you understand the context you are working in, the better you will be able to lead change effectively. But that is very difficult for most of us. All of us know a person who has laser-like vision when it comes to one area of expertise, say IT, HR, or finance. They are great at showing you what's not working in that area and suggesting ways to fix those problems, but they miss other cues. I recall one organization that branded one person on the team "the quality guy" (and that was not a compliment). When he spoke, people expected him to link every topic to quality improvement. Not that people didn't agree with him about the importance of quality improvement, they just thought that he missed the importance of other burning issues, like how will we service the debt next month?

Participants in a study were asked to watch a video of two groups on a basketball court. One team was dressed in white and the other in black. Participants were asked to count the number of passes the team in white made. While they watched the video, a woman with an umbrella walked through the center of the court. Only about 20 percent noticed her. When another group of participants in the study watched the video without being given a task, everyone saw the woman with the umbrella. The phenomenon is called selective looking. (In a similar experiment, a man in a gorilla suit moonwalked through the scene with similar results.)[2]

Many plans for change emphasize the financial issues. Others give a lot of attention to the technical side of the change. Others put a strong emphasis on the human issues associated with the change. So, you might think that it would be a good idea to make sure your plans included strategies for dealing with financial, technical, and human issues. And, of course, you would be correct, but you'd still be missing a big piece—and that's context.

Many organizations support narrow thinking. They hire people to fill specific roles. Of course that makes sense, but it does create fiefdoms of expertise. As these people work together, they have their unique world-views reinforced. And when it comes time to lead change, their own knowledge and comfort is where they focus their attention. They miss the woman with the umbrella.

W. Edwards Deming, a guru of the quality movement in Japan and the United States, said that over 90 percent of all performance problems were systems problems—and not the fault of individuals. Yet, individual performance management plans persist like summer colds.

Focusing on individual performance permeates much of what we do. When we read mysteries, we look for "who done it." In sports, we want to know who was the MVP (Most Valuable Player) in Sunday's big game. In the world of business and politics, we want to know who to applaud and who to blame. And, of course, a hero can turn into a villain overnight.

But this attention on the individual or the single cause for success or failure misses the point. Everything happens in context.

BAD APPLES OR BAD BARRELS?

In 2004, the Abu Ghraib prison scandal broke. Pictures appeared of laughing prison guards torturing prisoners. We wanted to know how this could happen. And who was responsible. We found her. Her name was Specialist Lynndie England. She was photographed holding a leash that was attached to a prisoner lying in a hallway. Specialist England, along with approximately eleven others, were court-martialed. England and one other soldier were sentenced to prison while others received dishonorable discharges. The general in charge was demoted to colonel.

Noted social psychologist Philip Zimbardo was interviewed on CNN. The interviewer suggested that perhaps this scandal was just the case of a few bad apples. Lombardo said the problem wasn't just a few bad apples, it was the barrel that was bad.

The dozen or so people who were punished were considered the bad apples and the scandal went away. Anyone thinking of building and running prison camps in another country would do well to take Lombardo's words to heart. It's the barrel. If you build the same type of barrel, you are likely to get similar results.

Great organizations all tend to be pretty much alike in some fundamental ways. They've got good barrels. Now, look at the context of your organization. That unique barrel creates conditions that support particular types of behavior. The context you are leading in makes a huge difference.

"But what about standards?" I hear you cry. Of course we need to have standards. There are bad apples, and often that's where we look first—but then we stop looking. I visited a plant that manufactured cell phones. People there successfully initiated a grassroots-led employee involvement program that enjoyed stunningly good improvements in quality and productivity. I talked with one of the workers on the line and asked if there were people on the floor who didn't buy into the program and continued to treat the work as a nine-to-five drudge. He said that group probably made up about 5 percent of the employees. But he went on to say that if they paid too much attention to that small group, they would divert themselves from supporting the 95 percent who were doing great work.

So how do we do both: pay attention to what's in front of us and pay attention to the overall context, all at the same time? How do we know when to ignore the lackluster performance of the 5 percent and focus on the other 95 percent?

Monovision contact lenses allow the wearer to see things at a close range out of one eye and see distance out of the other. We need something like these lenses when we look at our organizations. We need to be able to look at the big picture and the details almost simultaneously. Over the years, I found the monovision contacts analogy has helped keep me from getting too enamored with the picture I was seeing out of one eye.

In order to be adept at seeing out of both lenses, we need to know how the world can look through each, or we will continue to rely on the familiar way of seeing things. I will assume that most of you are pretty good at seeing what's in front of you. You pick up on the details. You can pinpoint good and bad performance. You can find mistakes in the ledger. Isolate a glitch in the production process. Find the hole in a planning process. That description is true of most of my clients.

The next section examines how to use the other—less familiar—lens, the one that can see context.

LOOKING AT THE CONTEXT

Often people who try to describe chaos theory use the analogy of how a butterfly flapping its wings in the Amazon could have an impact on weather in Seattle. In other words, changing weather conditions can come from anywhere. They aren't suggesting that we find that stupid butterfly and get rid of it, but that many things from anywhere could have an impact on weather in other parts of the world. You can't tell exactly where it is going to come from or when or why. It's chaos. The commission that studied the Shuttle Columbia disaster understood this.

Looking at the context for a change in an organization is a lot like that. Support, opposition, new threats, changing conditions in the marketplace, etc. can impact your change. Things seemingly can come out of the blue that bolster your change or threaten it. That's life.

You can be a great leader, the stuff of legends, but context can do you in. On the other hand, you may never have seen yourself as much of a leader, but conditions change. You rise to the challenge, and to your surprise, you are excellent. Who would have ever predicted that Abraham Lincoln would have been considered one of the U.S.'s greatest presidents? If you had looked at his limited public service and his modest small-town legal practice, it would have been hard to imagine him ever rising to the challenges of the presidency as the United States was being torn apart.

No matter how much I write in this chapter, I couldn't possibly cover all there is to cover, for one simple reason—we can't know all the forces that could have an impact. But we can tend to the major contextual cues, and that can increase the odds in our favor.

I divided looking at context into three major categories:

- Organizational Culture as It Relates to Leading Change
- Shifting Surroundings
- Your Mindset as the Leader

Organizational Culture as It Relates to Leading Change

"Behind every managerial decision or action are assumptions about human nature and human behavior."[3] Those words were written by Douglas McGregor in 1960. They still serve as a helpful guide to finding out what an organization and the leaders in that organization value.

You might wonder why I would choose to focus on studies that were done decades ago. In business book terms, that's almost pre-Guttenberg. Well, when I went back to McGregor's original writings I was struck with how well they captured business today. Granted, organizations look different today. They say different things. Everyone knows to talk about how "the team did it," how "we are all one family," and yet, scratch the surface and you find Theory X and Theory Y still at play. Welcome back, Douglas McGregor.

His work gave me the foundation I needed to look at what supports an environment of successful change. I am indebted to McGregor's work for my riffs on his thinking: Theory X in Sheep's Clothing and the Creation of Misleading X's.

McGregor suggested that there were two quite different sets of assumptions that drive the actions of those in charge: Theory X and Theory Y.

In McGregor's own words, those who think Theory X is a true statement about human nature believe:

1. The average human being has an inherent dislike of work and will avoid it if he can.
2. Because of this human characteristic of dislike of work, most people must be coerced, controlled, directed, threatened with punishment, to get them to put forth adequate effort toward the achievement of organizational objectives.
3. The average human being prefers to be directed, wishes to avoid responsibility, has relatively little ambition, wants security above all.[4]

Others believe in Theory Y. As McGregor put it:

1. The expenditure of physical and mental effort in work is as natural as play or rest.
2. External control and the threat of punishment are not the only means for bringing about effort toward organizational objectives. Man will exercise self-direction and self-control in the service of objectives to which he is committed.
3. Commitment to objectives is a function of the rewards associated with their achievement.
4. The average human being learns, under proper conditions, not only to accept but to seek responsibility.
5. The capacity to exercise a relatively high degree of imagination, ingenuity, and creativity in the solution of organizational problems is widely, not narrowly, distributed in the population.
6. . . . [T]he intellectual potentialities of the average human being are only partially utilized.[5]

Theory X conjures up a world that Charles Dickens knew: sweatshops and hellholes. It is the world of micromanagement and distrust of others from top to bottom.

A book on leading change in a Theory X environment might suggest that you need to tell people what to do and monitor their work closely because there is no guarantee that any work will get done without your watchful eye. The book would go on to advise that you need to use any means at your disposal to get people to do what you expect them to do. Skills at threatening, punishing, manipulating, and terminating employees are critical to your success. And the book's dedication would likely be to Machiavelli.

The philosopher Jeremy Bentham (1748–1832) wrote about a workplace where a supervisor would sit high atop the manufacturing facility and view the work of everyone, so that anyone could be monitored at any time. Leaders who subscribe to Theory X would love that approach to supervision.

Theory Y conjures up another world. Think about any of the major business books over the past couple of decades that celebrate well-run companies, and you most often see the world of Theory Y in action. Just look around you and you'll see companies that expect a lot and treat employees at all levels with dignity and respect. My favorite description of this is Nordstrom's legendary employee handbook which reads in full: Use your best judgment at all times. In one simple sentence, they encapsulate the spirit of Theory Y.

TOOLKIT For a blank copy of a Theory X and Y assessment, visit www.askaboutchange.com and search for **Theory X and Y**.

All of the large system change approaches that encourage the active participation from all levels of the organization are based on the assumption that Theory Y is true.

It is easy to contrast a 19th century sweatshop with a 21st century organization that opens the books and encourages people to make decisions that affect the business. Given the nature of business books and most management training, you could be lulled into thinking that just by talking about trust, cooperation, and teamwork that you'd get the benefits of a Theory Y culture. Beware.

Theory X in Sheep's Clothing

Leaders know how to hide their true beliefs. And in many instances they will not even allow themselves to see their own deepest beliefs about what motivates other people. Here is a corporate values statement:

> *Respect:* We treat others as we would like to be treated ourselves. We do not tolerate abusive or disrespectful treatment. Ruthlessness, callousness, and arrogance don't belong here.

> *Integrity*: We work with customers and prospects openly, honestly, and sincerely. When we say we will do something, we will do it; when we say we cannot or will not do something, then we won't do it.

Inspiring, huh? Sounds like a great Theory Y place to work until we realize that this was part of Enron's values statement.

Creating the Misleading X

Theory X assumptions whether obvious or hidden do something quite dangerous. They create Misleading X's.

Treating people like they aren't responsible and can't make adult decisions breeds Theory X behavior. We might say we believe in Theory Y (see the Enron values statement), but act as if Theory X were true. And, when we do, we create the conditions for the type of behavior we were trying to avoid. It's rather ironic and sad.

If you look around and see people who take little initiative, who don't seem at all motivated, definitely don't want to get engaged, don't volunteer, and don't stay late unless extra hours means time and a half, you could jump to the conclusion that Theory X assumptions were true. Or that your organization had the misfortune to hire all the lazy, good-for-nothing people in the tri-state area. On the other hand, you might be witnessing employees' responses to how they are treated. You just might be part of an organization that practices Theory X behaviors and might have created a workplace of Misleading X's.

There is one very easy way to tell. If people enter your doors with enthusiasm on the first day at work and within months look like they are attending a cast party for *The Night of the Living Dead*, you are probably creating a culture of Misleading X's.

You, as a leader, could be part of a management team that builds and maintains that bad barrel.

There is a powerful concept in psychology called social proof. We go along with things because everyone else does. According to Robert Cialdini, "What is easy to forget, though, is that everybody else observing the event is likely to be looking for social evidence, too. And because we all prefer to appear poised and unflustered among others, we are likely to search for the evidence placidly, with brief, camouflaged glances at those around us."[6] So, if no one is concerned, there must not be anything to worry about.

When I work with individual leaders, I find that their values and hopes for others are often in the Theory Y camp, and yet they are part of management teams that support practices and behaviors that look suspiciously like Theory X. I think social proof may be at play. You look around. Rick doesn't seem worried. In fact, no one looks worried that we are building a Puritan-styled dunking stand in the courtyard for people who miss deadlines. So you think, "If no one else is worried, then maybe it's not as bad as I thought."

Where Are We: Theory X or Theory Y

There is hope. Since most people like the assumptions behind Theory Y, if you can begin to change the culture to one that is a bit more humane, you could see significant shifts in behavior. People crave being treated with dignity and respect.

I invite you to answer these two questions:

- Where is my organization on a continuum from Theory X to Theory Y?
- What do I believe? (Do I believe Theory X describes most human behavior, or do I believe that Theory Y is a better description of people where I work?)

What to Look For

Here are some things to consider as you decide if you and your organization lean toward Theory X or Theory Y.

Exclusive to Inclusive Decision Making. Ask yourself, how do decisions really get made? Forget about the values statement hanging somewhere in your office. Forget about phrases like "respect for all opinions" and "teamwork is our goal" and take a look at how people truly make decisions.

Does the most senior person make the decisions? Who has the power to say yes or no? Think about what happens when someone other than the top person comes up with an idea. What happens to that idea? Are there unwritten rules about who can talk about certain subjects? What happens when someone disagrees with the position of the person or group in charge? Obviously, a Theory X organization is likely to act out of a command and control culture, holding decision making authority close.

Micromanagement to Delegation. A Theory X organization needs to control everything. Management needs to watch over work at its most minute detail à la Jeremy Bentham. A Theory Y organization is far more likely to trust people and delegate authority and responsibility wisely. That doesn't mean they delegate to everyone, but once a person proves that he or she can do the job, they decrease close management and delegate more fully.

Fear to Trust. Are people afraid to speak up and tell the truth as they see it? Or, do they feel trusted and trust others in return?

Hold Critical Information Close to Opening the Books. Who has access to the information that drives the business? Do the executives closely guard financial data as well as information about strategic direction, or does your organization open the books and allow everyone to see the numbers and trends that shape where you are headed?

Paternalism to Adult/Adult Relationships. Even though paternalism may seem like leaders care, it is the concern of those in power for their underlings. Noblesse oblige. The leaders will take care of the little kids. This type of relationship saps initiative and can cause reactions against the overly protective and emasculating behavior of leaders.

Needless to say, the first words in each of these categories defines Theory X: exclusive decision making, micromanagement, fear, hold information close, and paternalism. And Theory Y is marked by the terms: inclusive, delegation, trust, open the books, and adult-to-adult relationships.

The first question: Where is your organization?

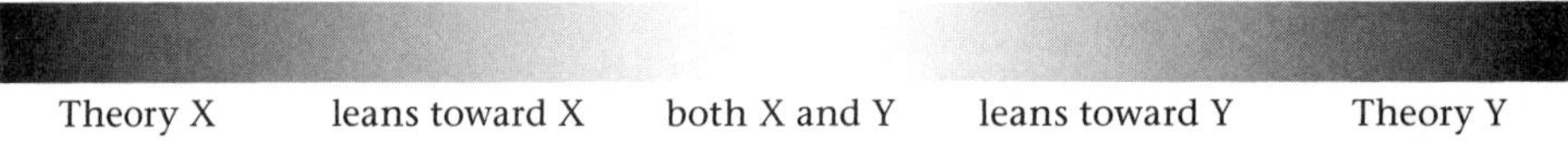

Theory X | leans toward X | both X and Y | leans toward Y | Theory Y

Second question: Where are you with regard to your belief about what motivates people?

Interpreting the Scores

X/X (Your organization values X and so do you.) It's not likely that you'd be reading this book if you scored yourself an X who works in an X environment. But just in case you are still reading, it looks like you've found a perfect home. Your values match the organization's. Unfortunately, it will be very difficult to build support for change since people will be suspicious of any effort to involve them. The best you probably can hope for is compliance. Don't expect commitment. People are not likely to go the extra miles needed to make a project a success.

Both X&Y/Both X&Y (Your organization is mixed and so are you.) You and the organization probably pigeonhole people into boxes. Maybe certain groups get Theory Y treatment, others get Theory X. Some old union-management organizations considered the union to be Theory X and management to be Theory Y. I have seen class, race, gender, what college you went to, and rank in the military (even if you were in a civilian organization today) be the grounds for making Theory X or Y assumptions about groups of people. If you find an X/Y split, it will be difficult to build support throughout the organization because you won't trust what you hear from the groups you believe are Theory X.

Y/Y This is ideal for the types of change that engage people. You believe in people's intrinsic motivation and the organization encourages practices that get the best from people. So, why are you wasting time reading this book? Go out and do something with these people!

X/Y (The organization values X, you value Y.) This is a very common and very difficult split. This chapter on context is written for you. You've got to know the territory that you are working in. You can't assume support for your ideas. You must do everything you can to demonstrate to those in power that your efforts to involve people really make sense. You may need to do small pilot tests so they can see for themselves. Maybe conduct a single Kaizen or other quality improvement event on an issue that is important and where you believe you can demonstrate tangible success. You need to be strategic. You can't afford to make a mistake. Your bosses and sponsors probably won't forgive you and give you a second chance.

Ask yourself, can I shine—do my best work—in this environment? If not, it may be time to leave. Though it is possible, it is unlikely that one person (unless you have amazing credibility and power) will be able to turn a Theory X organization around.

Y/X (The organization is Y and you are X.) You poor little puppy, life has got to be tough on you. All these touchy-feely get-people-involved initiatives just take away from getting the work done, right? Who are these people? You probably agree with the comedian Emo Philips who once said, "Real men don't have souls." You are working in the wrong organization. Even if you are successful at forcing a change through, you very well could develop a bad reputation in the process. Unless you want to dramatically change your mindset to one that gives people more of a chance to act like self-motivated adults, you will be pushing a rock and your career uphill.

What If You Believe Theory X Is True

Let's say you lean toward Theory X assumptions about people. You do have options.

1. Don't take on the challenge of leading changes if your organization leans toward Theory Y. If you do, you'll set yourself up for trouble. Odds are that you will fail, so why do that to yourself?
2. Find a Theory X place to work. They do still exist. And surprisingly, some of them can attract and keep very talented and motivated people by offering them lots of money. It's as if they were saying, "Give me all that you've got and when you turn 55, we'll make you rich beyond your wildest dreams." Some of these organizations do quite well, but my informal poll suggests that many more of them fail.
3. Finally—and the option I hope you might consider—you can change your mindset. Really, you can. You've got to want to, but it is possible. More about mindsets later in this chapter.

What If You Believe Theory Y Is True

Let's say that you are a Theory Y leader working in an organization that leans toward Theory X. You've got options as well.

Option 1. You can lead with the hope that the organization will appreciate your innovative approach to working with others. And after the applause dies down, others will wipe tears from their eyes and promise to help in any way they can.

This is a dangerous approach but one that lots of well-meaning leaders take. It looks good on paper and in the movies, but your real life is more like the sitcom *The Office* or the movie *Office Space*. If you build it, don't bet on them coming. Odds are that you will fail. Please don't choose this option.

Option 2. You can turn down the opportunity to lead this change. Sure it may cost you, but so will your failure to deliver the change they are looking for. Years ago, Fram ran a commercial that advertised its oil filter. It showed a mechanic standing under a lift. Apparently the car was in for major work. The mechanic held up a $10 oil filter and said, "You can pay me now or you can pay me later."

Option 3. You can add the need to build support to your to-do list. You'll need all the support you can get since the culture is going to be working against you. Identify who must support you and then begin to develop strategies to earn that support. And move cautiously. Make sure you don't get out ahead of your sponsors and other stakeholders on the Cycle of Change.

Shifting Surroundings

The environment is the air you breathe. The quality of that air has an impact on most of what you do. When runners trained for the 1968 Olympic games held in Mexico City (2,309 meters or 7,575 feet above sea level), they prepared by running in higher elevations. They knew that being a great runner at sea level would not be sufficient to win in thinner air. They understood the context.

And here's my last sports analogy (in this chapter): Think of the American version of football. The coaches plan a series of plays designed to capitalize on the team's strengths and the opponent's weaknesses. All week long the team practices those plays. But early in the first quarter, the star quarterback pulls a hamstring and can't play the rest of the game. And the opponent decides—without consulting you—to shift its own offensive strategies this week. Instead of a running offense, they introduce a sophisticated passing game. Suddenly, those wonderfully rehearsed plays don't make so much sense. You've got a new game on your hands. Do you use the plays you've been practicing all week or do you recognize that conditions have changed and adapt?

Of course you try to adapt. The same is true when you lead change. You plan based on one set of assumptions, but those may change even before you get started. It's that butterfly flapping its wings again.

There are some parts of the environment that you can anticipate and others you can't. But the more you know about your environment (like the elevation for the event is a mile-plus above sea level), the easier it will be to adapt as needed.

A few examples might help.

- You are a defense contractor and the federal government decides to make a significant shift in how it allocates resources. This decision wasn't even on your radar screen two weeks ago, but some legislator saw an opening for a new plant in his district, and now you are scrambling.
- You own a car dealership. Your customers love you. Most of your sales come from repeat business and word of mouth. Things just

couldn't get better than this. And then you hear on the news that the manufacturer of the cars you sell has allowed unsafe cars to be sold for years. This news report grows. The government gets involved and suddenly your reputation and sales plummet.

- A major foundation that supported your nonprofit theater for years decides to shift most of its grant money to educational institutions. From $1 million a year, you are now going to get $100,000 next year.
- You offer cell phone service around the world. Then Google decides to manufacture its own phones and allow people to buy from them and select their own plans. It's a new marketplace.
- You manage all of your company's DVD rental places in a large metropolitan area, and then Netflix comes on the scene. They seem to have everything in stock. No late fees. Customers can return DVDs by putting them in the mail. As you prepare to meet that challenge, Netflix starts to offer movies online.
- OPEC decided to control the flow and therefore the price of oil from the member countries in the early 1970s. Almost no one saw it coming except Royal Dutch Shell. They had engaged in a scenario planning process in which they envisioned things that could possibly happen in the future. One such scenario speculated that OPEC would become a powerful force. Shell's competitors were caught napping. The American auto industry didn't appear to see it. But Shell's ability to pick that scenario off the shelf allowed them to move from a relatively small oil provider to one of the largest in the world.

> **TOOLKIT** For a podcast on the value of scenario planning, visit www.askaboutchange.com and search for **scenario planning**.

The Usual Suspects

Here are some things you probably already pay attention to when you consider a major change:

- What's the current business environment and what changes do we anticipate or even imagine could happen over the coming months and years? What are the potential threats? Potential opportunities?
- How might the demographics of our customer base change over the coming months and years?

- Will there be a need for what we offer two years from now?
- Is there anything in the mood of our customers or potential customers that seems to be shifting?
- How about the demographics of the next generation of workers? Will we be able to hire the level of talent we need at a cost we can afford?
- What assumptions do we make about the value we offer?

This sounds a lot like a strategic planning SWOT analysis (strengths, weaknesses, opportunities, and threats). That can be a good way to imagine possible things that could happen, but it is important that you push the boundaries of those conversations so that people think and talk about the unthinkable. You know, those painful "what if this happened . . ." types of questions. About 55 percent of people die without a will. We don't like talking about the inevitable, let alone the bad things that might happen. As a leader, you need to push yourself and your colleagues to ask tough questions about your environment and forces at work in it. If you have any culture surveys or models around, those items are often worth adding to your scan of the usual suspects.

The Unusual Suspects

Here are some things that may be important and yet probably are not part of your typical SWOT scan of the environment:

- How might the political climate globally or in our country impact what we do and how we do it? (It could be unrest in some part of the world or a change in administration in our own country.)
- How resilient are the people? Daryl Conner used this term in *Managing at the Speed of Change*[7] to call our attention to the fact that sometimes the idea can be good but people are worn out. (By the way, Conner may have been the first to treat resistance to change as a serious issue and not relegate it to simplistic "you scratch my back, I'll scratch yours" tactics.)
- What's the history of changes like the one we've got planned in our organization? Do people look on these types of endeavors positively or negatively?
- Are there other things going on in the organization that could distract people from fully committing to this new initiative?

- Are there predictable things that we already know will grab people's time and attention?
- Are there any other projects in the works that could compete with ours for people and resources?
- How capable are we at imagining worst-case scenarios? Think of Royal Dutch Shell and OPEC.

And maybe the hardest unusual suspect to keep in mind is: multiple realities. When you mention a particular new project, everyone will see it through his or her own eyes and interpret it using lenses that have been honed over a lifetime. Their Level 1 interpretation of "facts" could be significantly different from yours. Their Level 2 emotional reaction could be quite different as well. And your view of their trust in you may be shockingly different (Level 3). Their view of *their own world* as it is today is 100 percent accurate in their own mind's eye. (Just as your view of current conditions is 100 percent accurate in your mind's eye.)

Remember the butterfly in the Amazon? Anything could shift how people see things and how they react. Imagine that Chris's uncle got laid off when a similar organization in another city went through a change that sounds suspiciously like the one you've got planned. Chris, being the maven that he is, tells others. They spread the word. And soon there is a viral reaction before you even schedule the first meeting. Not only could this happen, it occurs all the time.

Your Mindset as the Leader

There is a story attributed to Carl Sandburg. A stranger walks into a town and asks a guy sitting on his porch what people are like in this town. The guy says, "Let me ask you, what were people like where you came from?" The stranger tells him that they were mean, spiteful, and just no-good. The guy on the porch replies, "Funny, that's just what you're going to find here too." Later in the day, another stranger walks into town and asks the same question. The guy on the porch responds by asking what people were like where he came from. The stranger said, "I hated to leave. They were the nicest people in the world. They'd give you the shirt off their backs." The guy on the porch replies, "You're in luck, that's just what you'll find here too."

Mindsets make a huge difference in how we work with others. "Mindsets frame the running account of what's taking place in people's heads," says Carol Dweck, a professor at Stanford and a leading researcher in this area.[8] She has found that people tend to either have fixed mindsets or growth mindsets, and those worldviews are radically different from each other.

The fixed mindset is "a fixed ability that needs to be proven" and a growth mindset is one "that can be developed through learning."[9] She suggests that Enron, as a corporation, had a fixed mindset. It hired very bright people and paid them well. So far, so good. But Dweck writes that Enron worshiped talent "thereby forcing its employees to look and act extraordinarily talented . . . it forced them into fixed mindsets. . . . We know from our studies that people with the fixed mindset do not admit and correct their deficiencies."[10] She suggests that Ken Lay, the founder, chairman, and CEO of Enron, looked down on those below him, treating them like serfs, including the company president who seemed to be one of the few (if not the only person) to wonder if they were headed down the wrong road.

People with fixed mindsets need to be *the* star.

A growth mindset is quite different, it thrives on challenges. It believes in learning— picking yourself up after a fall, figuring out what went wrong, and trying again. If Enron had been built on the beliefs behind a growth mindset, it still might have hired bright and talented people and paid them well, but then it would have found ways for those same superstars to get even better. And that comes from practicing and learning from experience. To paraphrase the columnist Herb Caen, we begin to cut our wisdom teeth the first time that we bite off more than we can chew.[11]

Dweck points out that in every instance, the leaders that Jim Collins and crew studied in their profile of great companies[12] exemplified a growth mindset. In her words, "They were self-effacing people who constantly asked questions and had the ability to confront the most brutal answers— that is, to look failures in the face, even their own, while maintaining faith that they would succeed in the end."[13]

I think it is easy for us to see ourselves as being the models of a growth mindset when we may be nothing of the sort. Dweck writes that Ken Lay wanted to be seen as "a kind and thoughtful man." Even as his company destroyed the lives of many, he wrote to his staff, "Ruthlessness, callousness, and arrogance don't belong here . . . we work with customers and prospects openly, honestly, and sincerely."[14]

We want to believe that we encourage people to learn, grow, and be the best they can be. We want to be able to say that "ruthlessness, callousness, and arrogance don't belong" in our organizations. We may want to believe that, but our actions may indicate other beliefs that work against the very things we espouse.

In chapter 11, "Moving Toward Mastery," I suggest a way that you can begin to identify your own mindset a little more objectively than you might at first glance. Here is a hint: Think about a change that you led. Pick one that either went extremely well or was legendary in its failure. And then maybe with the help of a trusted advisor, consider what the beliefs might have been behind your performance as a leader.

For example, when I am asked what I value, I could easily sound like I was reciting the Boy Scout's credo. It's only in looking at my actual behavior that I begin to see the gap—sometimes a chasm between what I profess and what I do.

Robert Wood and Albert Bandura conducted a study using graduate business students, many of whom had experience in management. The task was to work on a critical management task. One group was "given a fixed mindset" and told that this exercise measured *their own* underlying abilities. The other group was told that management skills were built through practice and this task would allow them to develop those skills. The exercise was set up to be extremely difficult so that both groups failed the first few rounds. The students with a fixed mindset focus never learned from their experience and never improved. Those who were given a growth mindset focus kept getting better and better.[15]

In the classic (and sobering) article, "Pygmalion in Management," Sterling Livingston writes that people respond to how they are treated. "Some managers always treat their subordinates in a way that leads to superior performance."[16] He discusses a study conducted in a district of a large insurance company. Researcher Alfred Oberlander set up an experiment where he "observed that the outstanding insurance agencies grew faster than average or poor agencies."[17] As part of this study, an "average" unit was created. They predicted that this group would perform kind of so-so. But they didn't. "The assistant manager in charge of the group refused to believe that he was less capable than the manager of the 'super staff' or that the agents in the top group had a greater ability than the agents in his group."[18] He gave them a challenge to outperform the "super staff." Although they never achieved the numbers of the super staff, each year the so-called average group increased productivity by a higher percentage than the stars. Mindsets do matter.

BRIDGING THE GAP

Unless it comes naturally for you, force yourself to look at the wide array of forces at play in any situation. If you habitually look at individuals, force yourself to look at various groups, the full organization, and environmental factors as well. For now, just notice. This may not seem like a very productive thing to do, but it will be. You'll find that you will start to see situations differently. Instead of just seeing things as simple cause and effect, you will begin to see the richer tapestry. And those observations can breed understanding, maybe even compassion, and increase your options for responding. Obviously, you can't respond to what you don't see. Put another way, this "bridging the gap" exercise will allow you to begin to see the woman with the parasol.

Then begin to pay attention to your own mindset in various situations. Did you enter this week's planning meeting with an open mind? Were you willing to be influenced by others when they challenged you, or did you dig in your heels? Don't try to change anything, just notice. Do you see a pattern when you are engaged in leading change? Don't celebrate. Don't beat yourself up. Just notice. That's plenty for now.

PART II

Bridging the Knowing-Doing Gap

Remember the Rube Goldberg invention with the tripping man, moving rake, and a horseshoe propelled through the air? Like many change processes, it was way too complicated and risky. This section of the book shows you how to avoid creating plans that feel cobbled together. It also shows you what common pitfalls to avoid. (If you do nothing more than avoid those pitfalls, you will be doing much better than most change management strategies.) In addition, each chapter ends with suggestions on ways to bridge the knowing-doing gap.

6

How to Make a Compelling Case for Change

Action speaks louder than words but not nearly as often.

—Mark Twain

Many years ago I came up with a *brilliant* idea that could transform the organization where I worked. I was excited by the thought of what this idea could do for the people we served. I wrote a position paper—it was masterful—and sent it to the big boss. I didn't know him. He didn't know me, but he agreed to see me. As I presented my idea, he nodded and muttered a few condescending things. And then, rather abruptly, he said, "Well thank you, Mr. Maurer. You've given me lot to think about." And he might have added, "and don't let the door hit you on the way out." My pitch was over before it started. In hindsight, I realize he met with me just to get me off his back. He had no intention of considering this idea.

Over the years I found that I wasn't alone. I imagine many of you could tell a similar story. And as I turned my attention to large organizational changes, I saw that my experience was only a shadow of what could go wrong. No company went belly-up because my idea never got

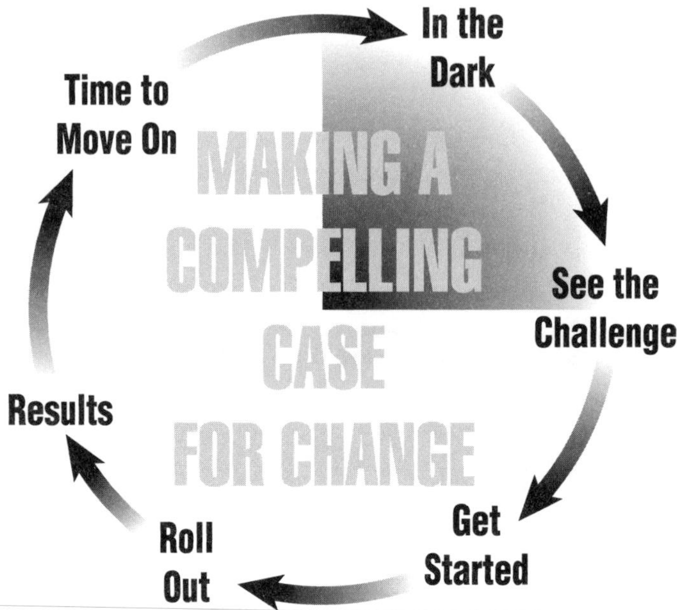

implemented. My career didn't hang in the balance. There were no missed opportunities that the organization now regrets. I got off easy.

WHAT MOST SUCCESSFUL CHANGES HAVE IN COMMON

One thing sets apart successful changes, new ideas, products, and services from those that don't achieve the desired results—people believe a change is needed. In an informal study I conducted in 2004, I found that in most successful changes, the people who needed to support the new idea felt a compelling need for the change. They understood why something new was necessary. In those changes that actually made matters "significantly worse," less than a quarter of the stakeholders saw a need for a change.

Making a Compelling Case for Change is critical to the success of your new initiative. If you fail to make a case, everything else is going to be much harder, and the chance of getting off track rises. The change will probably take longer, cost more, give you headaches, and ultimately fail. Making a case can be *that* critical.

But making a case is often overlooked. We can be in such a hurry to get moving and get things done that it is easy to forget this important part of the change process.

WHAT DOES IT MEAN TO MAKE A CASE FOR CHANGE?

People who are essential to the success of a change must believe that something needs to be done *now.*

It's not enough to understand that something must change, people must *feel* it. Making a Compelling Case is a combination of Level 1, Level 2, and Level 3 support. Your audience gets what you're talking about. They feel the urgency, and they trust the messenger.

Many use the image of seeing a burning platform to describe this stage of making a compelling case in the life of a change. It's a nice image but it doesn't go far enough. People need to feel the heat.

I have worked with clients along the shipping channel near Houston. There are derricks out in the water. Imagine I am sitting in an office with my client chatting and drinking coffee. Bob looks out the window and exclaims, "Look at that, Rick. That platform seems to be on fire." I ask, "Is it one of yours?" He replies, "No, that's a relief. Wait a second. . . ." He rummages through some papers and finds a phone number. He calls and alerts someone. He puts down the phone and says, "Well, that's done. Interested in lunch?"

Now imagine that we were standing on that platform and Bob said, "Hey, Rick, are your toes getting a little toasty?" That would have been a different experience and one that would have gotten our full attention. People need to experience the burning platform, not just see it.

> **TOOLKIT** For a copy of the Conditions for Change assessment, visit www.askaboutchange.com and search for **conditions for change**.

When you've really made a compelling case for change, people are ready to act. They begin to search for ways to correct the problem or seize the opportunity. They lead and they follow willingly. They want to correct this problem—or take advantage of this once-in-a-lifetime opportunity.

Senior managers in a financial services company didn't believe they needed to take the time to explain to employees the business challenge they were facing. The CEO disagreed. But she said, "I could be wrong. Would each of you take a few minutes and talk to four or five people in your departments over the next week and see how savvy they are regarding the challenges facing us?" At the next senior staff meeting the tone was significantly different. The executive team had learned a lot—they learned that the employees didn't know what was going on. That simple experiment on the CEO's part helped her make a compelling case to her executive team that they needed to begin to communicate critical information about the business to staff.

Her experiment gave the executives some vital information. They learned that people had no Level 1 understanding of the challenges facing them. And that got the executives worried (Level 2). They realized that they—the executives themselves—had to do a better job of communicating the need to change.

The head of environment, health, and safety for a plant needed the head foremen to see that there could be a big problem with their environmental practices. So, instead of repeating the government-sanctioned presentation on environmental policies complete with PowerPoint slides, he took a different course. He realized that they all had heard and probably could give that same presentation as well as he could. He knew this was not a Level 1 issue. He went around the plant and took photos. During the meeting he showed these pictures, reminding people that he had taken them the day before. The first photo showed a huge chemical tank and tiny corroded spigot. It seems like everyone in that room collectively said, "Ohhhh." They knew the risk of a corroded spigot. As he went through the next few photos, you could see people leaning in. He had hooked them emotionally (Level 2). As for Level 3, they did trust him, but they didn't need to because the pictures spoke for themselves. They could have walked out of the conference room and verified if these were real or Photoshopped.

TOOLKIT For a podcast and an article on Open Book Management, visit www.askaboutchange.com and search for **open book**.

WHAT TO AVOID

Making a Case for Change seems so simple. After all, isn't it just common sense that we would make a compelling case before launching into planning? Unfortunately, the answer is no. As Mark Twain once observed, common sense isn't all that common. We do things that get in the way of even starting to make a case. Here are a few common pitfalls—things to avoid. If you aren't alert to them, they can jeopardize your case before you even get started.

Moving to How Before Why

People need to know why something is important before they can get interested or even be willing to hear how you want them to do it. Too often we fail to address why something is important before we launch into explaining how it should get done. I am not interested in the explanation of *how* until you've convinced me *why* this is important.

I have been subjected to many lengthy PowerPoint presentations when a well-meaning leader introduced a big change. The first three slides deal with why this change is important, and then the next 150 mind-numbing slides deal with how they are going to proceed. If he didn't grab their attention in those first three slides, he is not going to see a spark of recognition at slide 29. His audience tuned out twenty slides ago.

My Suggestion: Force yourself to give a presentation where you only show five slides. It'll hurt, but it will build character. It will force you to find other ways of engaging your audience. Like, you might try looking at them. Asking them questions. Things like that.

The Myth That All I Need to Do Is Tell Them

While presenting information clearly is important, simply explaining things does not grab people.

Level 1 is the lingua franca of the modern organization, but it's not enough. Just giving people facts and figures doesn't cut it.

It's as if you are thinking, "They've got to trust me on this." Just because you are the boss and have been around for a while doesn't mean that people necessarily trust you when what you say triggers powerful Level 2 emotional reactions. Because we feel the heat from the burning platform, we just assume that others will too. And because we are so comfortable putting slide shows together, we drown them in Level 1 data.

TOOLKIT For a podcast on the importance of why before how, visit www.askaboutchange.com and search for **why before how**.

But it gets worse. According to a McKinsey study, "What the leader cares about (and typically bases 80 percent of his or her message on) does not tap into roughly 80 percent of the workforce's primary motivators for putting extra energy into the change program."[1]

My Suggestion: Do what good actors do. Put yourself in others' shoes and imagine what the world looks like through their eyes. This may seem hard, but I do this exercise with engineers, IT folks, HR specialists, and managers of all stripes, and they can do it just fine. They begin to learn about the hopes, dreams, and fears of the people they want to influence. Give it a try. You can do it privately. It only takes a few minutes.

We're Late, We're Late for a Very Important Date

Like the Mad Hatter, it is easy to rush from one new project to the next, never building sufficient support for change. Then the next new thing is seen as merely the next "flavor of the month." And that is an invitation to resistance.

A large engineering firm starts many projects, but most of them die well before they see results. Consequently, managers and employees just roll their eyes when corporate rolls out a new idea. Some have the attitude, "This too shall pass."

My Suggestion: Take a breath. Slow down. Decide what's most important and then focus on that.

A Belief That You Can Force Them to Do It

No, you can't. People can find all types of creative ways to stop you in your tracks. For instance, the president of a small company once told me that his idea was dying due to "malicious compliance." People did just enough to stay out of trouble and keep him off their backs, but not enough to make the change a success.

There are a few exceptions to this. Some organizations bribe people with incredible bonus and retirement packages, so people will do anything to reach the pot at the end of that rainbow. But even that approach can have its problems. When these soldiers of fortune set priorities for their own work, your pet idea may not make it to the top of the list because it fails the "what's in it for me?" test.

Another problem is that the bribes usually don't reach down far enough into the organization, so the middle manager, professional staff, supervisors, and hourly workers don't have all that much interest in making the executives richer. What a surprise.

My Suggestion: Skip to chapter 11 and complete the "shift your intention" exercise on mindsets. It might help you focus on what's most important in making a case.

Taking Time Will Waste Time

Our research found that when people made a strong case for change, the rest of the project often went much more smoothly. In other words, they didn't face as much resistance, and things didn't get off track as often. Even though you believe that you are facing a crisis, you need to ask: Do others believe it is a crisis as well? If not, you've got a long slog in front of you. And the odds are not in your favor.

My Suggestion: Get a buddy who can keep you from moving so fast that you get out ahead of others and perhaps even yourself. Pick someone who has no problem telling emperors that they have no clothes on.

Making Them Learn Your Language

Old MIS (Management Information Systems) departments often had the reputation of speaking some foreign language when they worked with senior management and other departments. They made the critical mistake of speaking their own language and not translating so that their audience could understand them. It is your job to be "multilingual" so that various stakeholders can understand what you are saying. I have seen IT, HR, financial, and sales and marketing departments kill their own effort to make a case simply because they expected their audiences to learn their jargon. Big mistake.

My Suggestion: Take your presentation for a test drive. Try it out at home. And watch your audience's reaction. Ask them to raise their hands the moment they are confused. You don't need to dumb down your presentation, but you do need to speak so that you are understood.

Rely on the Three Most Common Ways of Communicating Change

Most leaders rely way too heavily on the big three ways of communicating change:

- PowerPoint
- e-mails
- memos

These have two major disadvantages:

1. They are all one-way communication tools. No opportunity for conversation, debate, dialogue. In other words, no chance for people to engage with you and chew on the material. It reminds me of a four-panel poster that showed a student's head being pried open.

Searching for Marco Polo

I was working with the leader of a government-wide improvement effort. As I told him the following Marco Polo story, he laughed. He said that he now realized why the most innovative and successful solutions were occurring hundreds of miles away in provinces far removed from the seat of government and daily scrutiny.

In 1980, Ford decided to improve the quality of its manufacturing process. Instead of making a grand executive pronouncement and trumpeting the change throughout the company, they started small. They searched for the Marco Polos of Ford—plant managers and union stewards willing to sign onto an adventurous journey without much of a map. When they found these Marco Polos, they invited them to pilot test quality improvement processes.

For three years, these test sites worked on quality improvement. Word got out—something different was going on at these locations. Interest built within the company. Once Ford had worked out the bugs and given others an opportunity to witness the test, they introduced quality improvement to the entire company. Test runs give people models. They can see whether it plays in Peoria. They can watch others implement the change. Getting a chance to see the change in action often dissipates concerns. However, it is important that the test site not be held up as something special or better than the rest. If that occurs, the rest of the organization is likely to dismiss the test.[2]

Sand was pored in, the head was resealed, and then the student was handed a diploma.

2. They all emphasize Level 1 information. People don't decide things based on Level 1 alone. Did you buy your last car based solely on what *Consumer Reports* said? I didn't think so. You've got to grab people emotionally too.

A good diet will recommend you use some foods sparingly. Consider these three resources to be the salt, sugar, and alcohol of your change strategy. Use them, but don't overdo it.

Force yourself to communicate information about this change without using any of the big three tools and see what happens.

WHAT IT TAKES TO MAKE A COMPELLING CASE

Find Out Where You Are Today

Think about a change you are considering today. Perhaps you are about to launch a new product, merge two departments, or fully automate the billing process. If it's a change that requires support and commitment from others, consider these three questions:

1. Does your own team feel an urgency to change?
2. Who else must feel a need to change?
3. What's the gap between what they see and what you see?

Question 1: Does your own team feel urgency to change?

You've Got to See the Same Picture

What do I mean by "seeing the same picture"? It's quite common for the group initiating a change to be in disagreement regarding the need. For example, the leader may feel a sense of urgency, and because of her power, others go along. This can create major problems later on, such as disagreement regarding priorities on budget and use of other resources. I recall a group of health care professionals who all held slightly different pictures of what was needed in the coming years. These different pictures led to different goals and priorities. And a lot of squabbles about where to put their time and money.

Listen Hard, and Dig Deep

Listen to various points of view. It is quite possible that members of your group have access to different types of data or that they interpret the same data differently. To paraphrase Yogi Berra, you can learn a lot just by listening.

Explore where you agree and disagree. Dig into differences of opinion. Different perspectives can offer insight on various facets of the issue. Take advantage of the resources on your team to give everyone (yourself included) a richer picture of the current situation.

It's essential that most members of your planning team see the same picture.

Talk to each other. (What a concept.) Here's what you might talk about:

- To what extent do we see a compelling need for change?
- Where do we agree—and where do we disagree?
- How can we come to agreement in a way that respects all points of view?

Be careful: don't dismiss listening hard in the mistaken belief that your entire team sees things in the same way you do. Too many teams avoid disagreements, causing individuals to work around each other using Machiavellian tactics trying to get their own projects up and running. Better to have the tough conversations early.

And a special warning to executive teams. The term "executive team" is an oxymoron in many organizations. These C-level men and women look like a team on the surface, yet they are anything but that. Their interests, rewards, and punishments for failure can be quite different. This creates a breeding ground for less-than-honest communication. I suggest you review chapter 5, "Ignore the Context at Your Peril." It may help you get a more comprehensive view of the pressures or support your executive team faces when you try to work together as a team.

Question 2: Who else needs to feel urgency to change?

It's one thing to make a case within your own group, it is quite another to make a case to all those who might have a stake in a change in your organization. Remember, in most successful changes, a majority of the stakeholders saw a compelling need for things to change.

Casting a wide net is essential. Many changes stopped moving forward because the leaders overlooked a critical group or individual. A software development company was six months into an internal change when the mailroom balked. And that brought things to a screeching halt. As one manager told me, "Who knew? Nobody even thought about the mailroom." Leaders weren't trying to snub the folks who sort the mail, they just didn't think of them. It is far better to cast a broader net than you think is needed instead of believing you are saving time and money by keeping the net near the boat.

Convene a short meeting. Invite a small group of people who understand the political dynamics of your organization. In other words, these people understand the context. Brainstorm who needs to see the necessity for this type of change. Be sure to include suppliers and customers in your sphere of who is important to your success.

- Who will this change impact?
- Who must support this change during the planning stages?
- During implementation?
- After the change becomes the new way of doing business?
- Whose money will we need?

I was working with a small project team in a large manufacturing company. I asked them to identify the stakeholders. Even though I was writing relatively small, I filled up two sheets of flip-chart paper. The team was surprised that so many groups and individuals would care about what they were doing.

Question 3: What's the gap between what we think those stakeholders see and what we see?

Perceptions Matter

What's the gap between the sense of urgency that you feel and what others feel? Although you don't need 100 percent of the stakeholders to feel the same degree of urgency, you do need a critical mass to feel the heat of the burning platform under their feet.

Pay attention to signals you've picked up that let you know where they are with regard to the need for this change. Are people saying, "It's about time," or do they still appear to be In the Dark. Are they saying things like, "There they go again," "What problem?" or "It's the flavor of the month."

Let's say you have no idea where a group or individual stands. And that happens a lot. We're all busy. Some of your stakeholders may be a continent away. Perhaps you've never met face to face. You could be in serious trouble. If you don't know these people well enough to know what they are thinking about critical business issues, you can't expect them to support you. It is in your best interest to find out what they're thinking as soon as possible.

Now you can use what you've learned to make a case.

Make a Compelling Case in Four Steps

The most compelling cases address Levels 1, 2, and 3. People understand what you're talking about, they literally feel why this is important to them, and they have confidence in the one delivering the message.

A company lost a major contract. Instead of trotting out the same old tired assortment of managers to give their budget projections, complete with tired clip art, they brought in someone from the contracting office of their former customer to tell them why they lost. You could hear a pin drop in that meeting. Not only did people get it—they could see why this loss could be just the tip of a dangerous iceberg. Once the case was made that something needed to change, then people could get interested in exploring ways to improve the work of their company.

This approach neatly combined information with an emotional wallop of bad news, delivered by someone who could have hired them. It covered Levels 1, 2, and 3 in a single package.

The four steps of Making a Compelling Case are built on the assumption that you did a good job of assessing where the people you need to influence are today. Without that knowledge, you'll be developing a plan without knowing your audience. Not only will you waste a lot of time, but your chance of succeeding will go way down.

Step 1: Review What to Avoid

Earlier in this chapter, I cover a number of things to avoid. Take a look at those and identify the ones that you need to especially watch out for. Underline them. Write them on your palm. Do anything to remind yourself that these tactics don't work.

Step 2: Ask Yourself a Question

The question is, "What do people need to know about this situation so that they'll slap their heads and say, 'We've got to do something right now'?" Don't try to figure out your strategy just yet. Start by identifying what they need to know that will have an emotional impact on them.

You could begin by noticing what got you so excited or concerned about the need for a change.

The following list might help you identify what will get people's attention:

- Trends that are having (or could have) a dramatic effect on your type of organization
- Your organization's great/dismal financial performance
- How your organization's performance compares to others in your industry or type of work
- Shifts in the demographics of the people you serve and the impact this might have

- Threats in the world such as terrorism and collapse of financial markets
- Dreadful or terrific customer satisfaction
- Quality or productivity data that make you shake your head with concern or delight

Now, think about how any of the items you selected might impact people emotionally (Level 2). Here are some of the common emotional reactions.

- It could cost me my job.
- It could reduce/increase my job security.
- It could result in lower stock performance.
- It could limit my career opportunities.
- This could mean losing members or customers.
- There are opportunities for me to learn, grow, or rise up in the ranks.
- I could make more money.
- I'd have greater opportunity to pursue my dreams.

You'll notice that the first list deals with rather global issues like changes in corporate quality or customer service, or things happening on the world stage. But the second list is made up of highly personal emotional reactions. That's typical of emotions. Initially, we get worried for ourselves and our families. We are aware of how global change hits us on a personal level first. How are we going to survive? Can I pay off my mortgage? Send the kids to college? What's in it for me? That's where you need to target your message.

What you say about how the company could benefit might be true, but you've got to connect those dots so that people realize you are talking about them. Without explicitly making those connections for people, you risk missing your audience.

Step 3: Brainstorm Ideas

Now that you know where your stakeholders are and what might grab their attention, go wild. Think about the possible ways to Make a Compelling Case. Here are some ideas:

- Consider approaches that have already worked in your organization. Ask yourself, why did they work? And could that strategy work in this instance?

- Hear from real live customers about what they want, what they like about what you do, and what they despise.
- Hear from real live *former* customers telling you why they took their business elsewhere.
- Talk with counterparts in similar organizations who have faced the same challenges and handled them well. Or perhaps they have a horror story to tell about how things went poorly. Consider a field trip to those organizations.
- Talk with—and listen to—people from around the organization as they tell about the challenges they face.
- Hear from an executive (or someone else) who your stakeholders respect deeply.
- Find alternative ways of providing data, such as photos or short videos.
- Open the books. Let people see what's going on without the glaze of interpretation and bullet points. If needed, help the stakeholders connect the dots and interpret the financial implications of what's going on today.
- Engage in personal chats. Hint: Your standing on stage with an audience of 300 is not a personal chat.

Step 4: Decide on Your Approach

Time to choose. Pick an approach (or approaches, for different groups). Practice. Get feedback. Practice some more.

Then do it.

Watch people's reactions. Remember, just because you make a presentation doesn't guarantee that others will be in awe. If they are less than moved by your stirring strategy, regroup and try something else.

You may be tempted to give up and move on to Getting Started on the Right Foot. Don't. If you move to "how" before addressing "why" to their satisfaction, you'll have a slow slog or a fight on your hands.

A general manager was exasperated. He could not get his management team to see the problem facing them. In a meeting, he blurted out, "Our plant is idle 40 percent of the time!" People gasped. With that single statement he did more than reams of spreadsheets had ever done to get people's attention. Being idle 40 percent of the time worried folks—and that's an emotional reaction. Sometimes our own mounting frustration (like "our plant is idle 40 percent of the time") can result in an action that gets people's attention.

Step 5: Reinforce the Message

People forget. After heart attacks many people start treatment programs, but only a few stick with the program so that they see the benefits that rehab could provide.

People are busy, and what's urgent today crowds out other important things. Plus we have a built-in immunity to change. (See an interview with the authors of the book *Immunity to Change* in chapter 11.) It's important to keep the message alive with the same emotional intensity you achieved at the outset.

During the reinforcement step, you can include some of the things I urged you to use sparingly in Step 2. Don't overdo it, but they can serve as good reinforcements for your message.

In addition, you might try:

- Broadcast voice mails

  When Continental Airlines worked their way back from bankruptcy years ago, the chairman, Gordon Bethune, sent out broadcast emails regularly to every employee to thank them and let them know what was going on. He did not delegate this task. People heard his voice.

- Question-and-answer sessions

  Town hall meetings and virtual town hall forums can be great places for people to get answers to questions. And they are great ways for you to learn where people are currently with regard to the change.

  Two warnings: If you are someone who gives a twenty-minute response to a simple question, ask someone to facilitate and keep you in line. I have seen many well-intended town hall meetings die simply because the leader couldn't shut up. And know your own knee-jerk reactions. Know what might trigger an outburst of some sort from the group and practice what you'll do to make sure you don't give in to the jerking knee.

- Management by wandering around

  Tom Peters and Robert Waterman[3] found that many good leaders just wandered around with no agenda. Once people got used to this and saw that the leader was there to learn and to answer questions when possible, people opened up.

I had a client who moved to a new lab down the hall. I asked how work was going. She said great. Her new boss always seemed to know what was going on and was a conduit for her and others to get information and resources. I asked how he did that. She told me that he leaned up against the wall, drinking coffee, at the place where the two hallways intersected. It was a perfect place for people to engage him and for him to engage them.

BRIDGING THE GAP

First, you've got to decide why there's a gap between what you want to be able to do and what you're doing today. Consider these five possible reasons for a gap.

Slap-Your-Head Obvious Solution

Imagine that you read the list of "things to avoid" at the beginning of this chapter and saw yourself. With a blinding flash of insight, you realized what you could do differently. (Isn't it great when it happens that way?) When that occurs, it's pretty easy to turn knowledge into action.

Lack of Knowledge

The thought that you need to make a case *before* announcing or planning a big change is unwelcome news for many leaders and often hard to understand. Many leaders find it hard to accept that most compelling cases are made when they both enjoy the trust of those who will be part of the change (Level 3) and believe that the need for change must grab people emotionally as well (Level 2).

Using the Cycle of Change and the three levels as lenses when you see others try to make a case for change may help emphasize the importance and complexity of making a compelling case.

Lack of Skill

Learning how to make a case that includes more than Level 1 facts and figures, and at the same time addresses Level 2 and Level 3 hopes and fears, can be a real challenge. It takes careful observation and deliberate practice. I find that with many of my clients, this is an area where coaching can be helpful. (Coaching can come from colleagues. But you may need someone to play the part of the child in "The Emperor's New Clothes" and tell you if your way of presenting the case is boring.) This might be an area where you turn to chapter 11, "Moving Toward Mastery," to get some ideas on ways to build your skills.

Competing Beliefs

This can be a tough one to recognize. In *Immunity to Change*, Robert Kegan and Lisa Lahey refer to this phenomenon as "hidden commitments." These are beliefs that work against your goals. For instance, you might truly believe that it is crucial to make a compelling case and at the same time believe that it is important to keep vital information about your business close to your vest. You can see how the desire to provide good information and the concern about revealing too many "trade secrets" can work against each other. Or you might believe that it is important for people to understand the opportunities and threats facing your business and, at the same time, believe that "knowledge is power." And you want to make sure you hang onto your power.

Context

You may believe strongly in being transparent and giving people critical information, but your organization doles out information on a "need-to-know" basis. If that's the case, you've got a choice to make. You can give in to the corporate culture, or you can find ways to make sure people are in the loop without putting your own career at risk. I know this can be a tough choice to make. I don't want to tell you what to do, but I can tell you that it is hard to find many major changes that succeed without stakeholders feeling that this big, new, potentially disruptive project is critically important to the organization.

Begin to notice ways in which you are influenced to act on something. You bought something you didn't expect to buy. You gave a donation to an organization you just learned about from a telemarketer. Notice what others do when they successfully make a case and get you to *buy* what they are *selling*.

Now the question is, how do you know you've made a case?

HOW YOU KNOW YOU'VE MADE A COMPELLING CASE

Experienced salespeople give this advice. Once you've made the sale—shut up! It's possible to undermine your case by talking too much. It's important to know when people are ready to change, so how do you know?

Listen for the Cues

Pay attention to what people are saying and how they are saying it. Listen for cues such as:

- People talk about "what *we* need to do" versus "what *they're* doing to us."
- People suggest ideas to deal with the problem or opportunity.
- People talk about why this change is critical to them. They explicitly address the "what's in it for me?" question.

Invite Questions and Comments

What can you do to encourage this kind of talk? Here are a few simple things to consider:

- Create opportunities for substantial give-and-take during meetings. Listen carefully to the types of questions and comments. Are people asking "why" questions or are they leaning in and suggesting "how" to proceed?
- Talk with people you trust who can give you "the word on the street." The eminent consultant Peter Block once said that the place you're more likely to hear what's going on is in the restroom, not in the meeting. Translation: Find informal places where you can talk with people.
- Ask people. Informally drop by people's desks or workstations and find out what they're thinking. Are they worried about the same things that worry you? Are they excited about the same possibilities? Do they see things that you might be missing?

Now it's time to get people involved in planning.

7

How to Get Started on the Right Foot

I have not ceased being fearful, but I ceased to let fear control me. I have accepted fear as a part of life—specifically the fear of change, the fear of the unknown, and I have gone ahead despite the pounding in my heart that says: turn back, turn back, you'll die if you venture too far.

—ERICA JONG

You walk into the large conference room and immediately see a banner that reads, "New Technology for the Future and Beyond." At your seat, you find a coffee mug with a logo emblazoned with that same inspiring phrase. You think, "Huh, what's this all about?" On the tables sit thick binders for everyone. You flip yours open and skim through a few pages. It all seems to be print copies of PowerPoint slides. Lots of white space and bullet points. So much for going green, you think.

Music starts. An off-stage announcer introduces your CEO, Charles "Call Me Skip" Heep. You check your BlackBerry, maybe there's something urgent you should be doing somewhere—anywhere—else. No such luck, so you settle in.

Skippy coughs into the mic and says, "Welcome everyone. I'm Skip Heep (he waits for applause). You may know me as your CEO (more applause). This is a big day for us. We are sitting on the cusp of an opportunity like

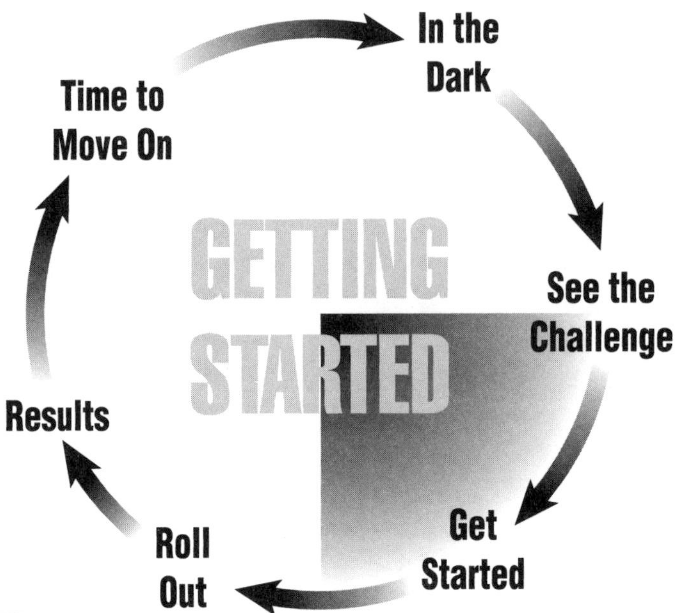

I've never seen before." You think, "We're sitting where? What's this opportunity?" Skip shows a few slides that must say something about this unique opportunity. Unfortunately you can't read that size font from this distance. (Note to self: get new glasses.) After a few minutes, Skip says, "OK, so I think you all see why I am excited to be part of this new direction for our company. I'd like to turn it over to head of IT, Phyllis Brotherly."

Phyllis asks everyone to turn to the first tab in their binders. You notice that there must be over a hundred pages of PowerPoint printouts behind this tab alone. You sigh. She begins her talk and doesn't end for a very long time. She asks if there are any questions. Silence, and then a few of the usual suspects ask some questions. Question four seemed like it might have been interesting, but you were tuned out for the first few minutes of her answer. Ah, well, maybe next time.

After the break, five more presenters explain what's what and how the company is going to make the dream of New Technology for the Future and Beyond a reality. A motivational speaker comes on to close the day. He tells you to be sure to have a good attitude. You think, "I wish I'd thought of that." Mercifully, it's 5:30 and you go home.

You've been to meetings like that, right? You may have run meetings like that. Sadly, these are where most changes actually start. A leader or a small cadre of senior people gets an idea in their heads. Their excitement builds. They put together a plan that explains where they want to go and how they want to get there. They give it an inspiring name. They hold a meeting to introduce the plan with lots of hoopla. If marching bands were still in style, one would be playing. People get coffee mugs, t-shirts, and obligatory binders. Who wouldn't be motivated by all of that?

Sometimes that approach works. But more often, it invites confusion and resistance.

It's like someone just flushed, sucking all the energy down the drain. And you know that next year those same leaders will conjure up another inspiring slogan and they'll be off and running again.

WHAT DOES IT MEAN TO GET STARTED ON THE RIGHT FOOT?

There is a better way to get started. Begin by making a compelling case for change so that people feel the need for change in their bellies. In other words, do the work of chapter 6, "How to Make a Compelling Case for Change." That's where change really starts. Get people out of the dark before you ask them to be part of a grand plan.

Imagine another room filled with a few hundred people. As you look around, you see people from all levels of the organization. You even see some of your suppliers and customers. As you sit down at your *assigned* seat, you find that you will be working at a table with eight or nine strangers. As you introduce yourselves, you realize that your table group is a microcosm of the entire organization. Interesting.

The meeting begins with a few short presentations coupled with conversations at your table about the need to change. You notice that very few people are using PowerPoint. You talk at your table about the challenges and opportunities facing you. A light begins to turn on: you see why this meeting is so important to the organization and to you personally. You're starting to learn stuff from people at different levels and in other departments. You're getting a richer picture of your organization and the challenges and opportunities it faces. You're hooked. You roll up your sleeves. You're ready to work.

Over the next couple of days you create and critique plans for addressing the challenges and opportunities facing you. Conversations move from elevated strategic discussions down to creating on-the-ground tactical plans. Sometimes things are intense, but in the end, civility wins out, and you come up with ideas that most can support.

By the end of the meeting, you have developed a plan that a few hundred people already understand because all of you created it. And not only that, most of you are committed to making it a success. What could have often taken months to do, you just accomplished in a few days.

For many of you reading this book, that story may seem unreal: the stuff of fantasy. For some others, that's the way you like to lead change.

Over the past fifteen to twenty years, pioneers in large systems change like Dick and Emily Axelrod, David Cooperrider, Kathie Dannemiller, Robert (Jake) Jacobs, Marv Weisbord and Sandra Janoff, and many others have created change processes that get people deeply involved and committed to the changes they help create.

If you are not familiar with approaches like the Conference Model, Appreciative Inquiry, Whole Scale Change, Real Time Strategic Change, and Future Search, I encourage you to check out any of these thoughtful processes for planned change. They all do a great job of addressing the challenge of making a compelling case for change first and then getting started on the right foot. (A good starting point might be *The Change Handbook*, by Peggy Holman, Tom Devane, and Steve Cady. It is a survey of over sixty such approaches!)

TOOLKIT For a brief description of some of the most popular large systems change approaches, visit www.askaboutchange.com and search for **large systems change**.

There is a lot to be learned from the pioneers of large organizational change approaches, even if you decide not to use the specific techniques.[1]

TOOLKIT For thoughts on large systems change in a virtual world, visit, www.askaboutchange.com and search for **virtual change**.

WHAT TO AVOID

The Getting Started stage gets botched more often than it gets done right. Here are some things to avoid that I've seen used to kick off a major change.

Too Much Focus on the Event

Some organizations put a lot of time and effort into creating gala events and then that's it. It's like buying some weights and a treadmill and then thinking that you've taken care of your need to exercise.

I have seen companies spend months and untold amounts of money planning these events. Lots of attention to getting the right speakers, the right graphics, a killer menu, a logo, and the gift bags. (Hint: There is no evidence that gift bags have ever motivated anyone to do anything.)

My Suggestion: Cato the Censor (234 B.C.–149 B.C.) once wrote, "Stick to the point and the words will take care of themselves." Remember why you are bringing people together, and then make sure everything you do is in service of addressing that single intention.

Let's say your purpose is "to engage a large diagonal slice of your organization in planning so that this project gets started on the right foot." That statement should become your mantra. Everything you do to plan the event must be focused on ways to meet that objective. If the VP of Whatshedo would like time on the agenda to talk about something unrelated to your purpose, be nice, but say no.

No Follow Through

Even well-intentioned high-involvement planning events can fail without follow through. Imagine you get people together. They work hard and develop a detailed set of guidelines to help implement this change. And then you drop the ball. Soon people forget about the plans they made, until the next change gets announced. And that next time, you will face a roomful of cynics who know that all you expect them to do is go through the motions.

My Suggestion: Only hold a planning event if you know for certain that you will do what it takes to lead this change through to completion.

The Wrong People in the Room

Just because you've got warm bodies in the room doesn't mean they are the right people to get the job done. They may be perfectly nice people, kind to their mothers and all that, but if they lack the knowledge, influence, or skill to help create a plan, that's a recipe for a pretty uneventful meeting.

My Suggestion: As I mentioned earlier, cast a wide net. Be sure to invite people who will be willing to speak candidly about their reactions to what's being planned. And make sure you invite people who represent a full range of interests and professional groups in your organization.

Confusing Attendance with Involvement

Showing people PowerPoint slides for seven hours and then asking, "Are there any questions?" is not involvement. It's important to not confuse giving information with planning. No one is planning anything (other than possible mutiny) while you are droning on through a set of slides. It is a rare slideshow that can engage an audience. So, realize that your presentation is probably only going to cover Level 1 informational issues. It is not likely to excite people (Level 2) or build people's trust and confidence in you (Level 3).

My Suggestion: If you want to give people a lot of information, write a book. Record a podcast. Send a series of tweets. Years ago, in a former life, a government agency asked me to write the script for a video that would introduce new employees to the rules and regulations of their organization. They handed me a bunch of manuals to guide my writing. I asked why they didn't just give these manuals to new employees instead of going to all the trouble and expense of making a video. They said if employees were forced to watch this video then they would know new hires had been exposed to the information. Don't do that to people.

Give People a Book

Lots of organizations give out books. For example, a lot of organizations have given executives and managers copies of John Kotter's *Leading Change* or James Collins' *Good to Great*, and both are great choices. Giving out those books would be fine if there was some concerted plan to do something with them. But it is the osmosis approach to leading change: Give 'em the book, they put it under their pillows, and voilà, they begin to lead with clarity and determination, making supporters wherever they go. Just handing people the book isn't likely to change a thing.

My Suggestion: Carefully choose the book you want to give out and then use it to guide planning and implementation throughout the organization. Don't give it out until you are certain that you want this book to be a bible for those involved in planning and implementing this new initiative. And know what you want people to do as a result of reading it.

Sheep Dip Training

I recall my Uncle Red dipping his hunting dogs in some foul mixture to kill fleas and ticks. He said that sheep farmers did the same thing with their flocks. Training can feel like that. Everybody gets dipped whether they need it or not.

You have probably attended courses that have included segments on change management. That's OK, but it's like that high school course you took ages ago that was supposed to do you some good someday. And now you can't remember a thing about algebra or second-year Latin.

My Suggestion: Only offer training when it relates directly to the change that you are about to start. Everything in that course should be focused on preparing people to meet the challenges of the change you are just beginning. That's how adults (and kids for that matter) learn. Otherwise, it may be interesting, but inconsequential.

Lacks Juice

Some change projects may be necessary but they bore people to tears. Designing new performance appraisal systems might fall into that category. Don't hold a big planning meeting that you know will only succeed if Starbucks supplies IV's for every table.

(Although I'd be happy if every performance appraisal plan went up in flames, most organizations seem to feel it's their duty to keep trying to improve these beasts.)

My Suggestion: For meetings that last more than an hour, only invite people to join you who are critical to the success of the change project. For all others, use surveys, focus groups, one-on-one interviews, but don't make them sit in a room for three days talking about something that they don't care about. For example, you could survey them on what they want from a change like this. What their concerns are. Ask if you can send them short documents for their feedback during the planning and implementation stage. And keep people informed. Let them know how you are using their input.

WHAT IT TAKES TO GET STARTED ON THE RIGHT FOOT

While techniques differ, there are some common themes running through the large system change approaches I alluded to earlier. All of them

- engage people deeply in the process, and
- provide a framework for developing a plan.

The principles that guide these types of changes—engage people and provide a framework for developing a plan—work just as well with a team of five as they do with a cast of hundreds.

Engage People Deeply in the Process

Once you determine who has a stake in this change, you need to decide the extent to which they should be involved in the planning and implementation. Many stakeholders want to be part of changes that affect their lives. Engage those people deeply. Create conditions so that they can influence the process and the outcome.

The change process is a real opportunity to increase the level of engagement in your organization overall and build strong working relationships, not only between you and the people you want to support you, but between management and labor, field and headquarters, and so on. Not only can involvement facilitate movement around the Cycle of Change, the process itself can begin to change how people work together. These types of large systems changes can begin to transform the culture you work in.

Other stakeholders may just want to be in the loop. As long as you don't mess with their sacred pet projects or ask too much of them, then keeping them informed may be sufficient. But keep your eyes open. Once you start planning, they may change their minds and realize that there is more at stake than they thought. If that happens, invite them into the process.

The challenge is to make sure you cast your net widely. Don't look to the usual suspects to help you, but brainstorm a list of all the groups and key individuals who might care deeply about this change. It is all too common for leaders only to enlist the help of people who already agree with them. Or only to think of those groups and individuals who they work with every day.

Provide a Framework for Developing a Plan

An effective planning process should include at least the items listed below in addition to getting people deeply involved. (You may find other themes that you need to address given your unique circumstance.)

Vision or Direction

A vision statement is what you want to occur at the Results point on the Cycle of Change. It is what you want to happen as a result of this change. (It makes no difference whether you call it vision, goals, or outcomes.) It is what you are shooting for. You should create that statement during the Getting Started stage.

TOOLKIT For an article on how to create a vision statement, visit www.askaboutchange.com and search for **create a vision**.

There is no one-size-fits-all approach to drafting such a statement or rules about what it should look like. I look for two things when I am working with my own clients:

Is it clear? Robert Mager, an expert on how to set goals and objectives, offered a simple and clear way to know if your goals are worth anything. "If you met the goal on the street, would you recognize it?"

Is it compelling? Do the people who need to work toward this vision feel that it is a worthy goal?

The same Level 1, 2, and 3 issues that must go into making a compelling case for change must go into the vision as well. "Is it clear?" is Level 1, of course, but the tone is all Level 2. And obviously, people need to believe that you are serious about this vision. That's Level 3.

Benchmarks Along the Way

Targets keep us on track and motivate us. In Edwin Locke and Gary Latham's research on motivation, they found that the single biggest motivator in the workplace was clear goals coupled with good feedback. Everyone should know where he stands with regard to progress toward these benchmarks along the way.[2]

Activity without goals and benchmarks is mushy business. It is hard for people to know what to do next. When that happens, they either create their own goals and direction or they lose interest.

I have seen organizations successfully use the "balanced scorecard" as a way for all to see where things stand at any moment. I have seen others use the "weekly huddle" developed by The Great Game of Business firm. A weekly huddle happens throughout the operation. People get together in groups and remain standing (which lets people know this is like a football huddle and the meeting will be tactical and short). They talk about specific targets they were trying to reach during the past week. Everyone reports on his or her progress and gives an explanation for where they are. This works best when people report a number such as sales, some quality measure, productivity, and so forth. No analysis. No judgment. The huddle breaks up and everyone goes back to work. It is effective because people want their numbers to be good and they don't want to let their fellow teammates down.

Address Competing Interests

I strongly believe that effective planning demands that we explore both sides of the polarity of support and resistance. Resistance can be fear (Level 2) or distrust (Level 3), but it can also be a concern that the proposed plan is not the best way to proceed and will harm activities that might make a positive difference.

TOOLKIT For a podcast on the value of de Bono's Six Thinking Hats model, visit www.askaboutchange.com and search for **Six Hats**.

People's competing interests—hopes, fears, other plans—must be taken seriously. Not to placate, but to explore and allow ourselves to be influenced by others. The plan should include ways to actively invite opposition. When people believe they have something to lose by this change, leadership's ability to work with resistance will be a critical factor determining whether the change will be a success or a failure.

Most often, organizations attempt to overpower or ignore resistance. This is often a tragic mistake. Include ways to keep the doors of communication open throughout the planning and implementation of the change.

One of my favorite techniques comes from Whole Scale Change and Real Time Strategic Change. (For a little more about these approaches visit www.askaboutchange.com.) When people are presented with a straw man proposal for a change, they are asked to identify what makes them glad, mad, and what they would add. While this may seem overly cute, I can tell you that it works well. It allows people to express their optimism (glad), their fear and resistance (mad), and suggest how they'd like to influence the plan (add).

Differences are real and need to be taken seriously. For example, imagine that your change involves the extent to which your organization would centralize its operations.

Here's what Barry Johnson, author of *Polarity Management*, said when I interviewed him a few years ago.

> Do we centralize to coordinate for system integration or do we decentralize in order to get close to the customer and empower people to be decisive on the front line? That is a polarity to manage. We need to be effective in our centralized coordination—and we need to be effective in our decentralized decision-making. If we can do both of those well—which are inherently in tension with each other—it will be beneficial for everyone involved in the system. It will be beneficial to those who are interested in the centralized coordination (usually the administration), and it will be beneficial to people who are on the front line because they feel like they've got an ability to be responsive to the customer and to use their own ingenuity and creativity.[3]

The change process needs to respect that there will always be a tension between field and headquarters. Barry Johnson might say that's life.

Let's accept the reality of that fact and create plans that would allow us to get the best from both ends of the polarity.

Contingency Plans

As much as you want your plan to be a success, spend some time exploring what could go wrong. One of my favorites is the "what if?" scenario.

Often the depth of the resistance doesn't even become apparent to us until we are asked to take action. For example, an administrative unit within a government agency was considering ways to improve efficiency. Their customers began to demand faster response time. The department's manual systems were no match for a clientele used to the speed of more modern systems. Although they faced resistance during the early stages of planning, it wasn't until the group began suggesting specific strategies that the deepest resistance surfaced. People who had supported the early planning became suspicious of the very strategies they had been supporting. It was not that they had been holding out, waiting for the right time to disrupt progress. It was just that as they got closer to implementing plans, they discovered factors they felt they had to resist.

The U.S. Army Corps of Engineers has developed a method to get issues out on the table before they become conflicts.[4] All the players involved in a construction project come together to define what this temporary partnership will look like. They discuss how they will handle such issues as quality, completion dates, costs and cost overruns, safety, and paperwork.

They address things that could go wrong. This is a pretty easy task; everyone in the business knows where the hassles are. Then they devise strategies for dealing with these potential pitfalls. Think of these as "what if?" scenarios.

Exploring what might happen is much safer than trying to tackle a problem when it is facing you. "What if?" scenarios allow you to step back and calmly play with possibilities without the risk.

Here are some things to consider:

1. If the groups have worked together before, identify projects where the groups were in conflict. If the groups are new, ask people to draw on their own experience to identify potential conflict over the change. Do not assign blame. The goal is to identify issues that could come up during the current change, not dissect the particular past events.
2. Form mixed groups with representatives from a cross section of departments and levels of the organizations involved. Have those

groups take on the issues identified in Step 1 and develop strategies to address these problems should they occur.
3. Have Subgroups report to the full group all questions, comments, and suggested changes.

Groups should address the following questions:

- How can we keep our focus on the goal if this issue occurs?
- How will we summon the courage to stick with it, even if the going gets extremely tough?
- What can we do to ensure mutual respect in the midst of this issue?

Kathie Dannemiller (1929–2003) was a founder of Dannemiller-Tyson, a consulting firm that specializes in helping organizations implement major changes. When Ford Motor Company wanted to begin building the new Mustang, they called her group in to assist. Here is how she describes the shift that took place when virtually all management and staff of the Dearborn plant—some 2,400 people—attended the conference.

> *It was on the third day and we had pulled everyone together to hear from the skunk works group. I asked the plant manager and the union president to each give a fifteen-minute "I have a dream" speech. "I have a dream for a Dearborn assembly plant that. . . ." The plant manager spoke first. At the end of the union president's speech, the plant manager said, "Al, we have the same dream! Let's do it together." They shook hands and then hugged. The whole room erupted in cheers.*
>
> *As we all walked back to the breakout rooms, I had the illusion that I was walking on air. I looked around and suddenly realized that there was hope.*
>
> ***That's** the shift. People could say, "No big deal. We can do this." These people believed that someone cared about them and cared about their plant.*[5]

When plant managers and United Auto Workers leaders hug, something is going on. This was not business as usual. A shift had taken place. Neither side has given up anything. The two leaders still had to answer to their constituents, but a shift had occurred that allowed them to see that they held similar dreams.[6]

- What can we do to ensure that all the critical issues get out on the table?
- How can we stay relaxed in the midst of this conflict?
- How can we promote the development of common values?

4. The whole group decides which of these strategies it can fully support.

Communication

Rather than delegating the writing of a communications plan to HR or the communications staff, ask your stakeholders three things:

1. What will they want to know along the way?
2. How often do they want to be informed?
3. How would they like to receive the information (e.g., meetings, blog posts, podcasts, voice mail, newsletters, face-to-face meetings)?

Once you know the answers, it is probably OK to delegate the writing of the communications plan and follow-up messages.

A warning: Of course, keeping people informed is essential, but you must create ways for them to keep you informed as well. Communication during change works best when people can influence each other. Be sure to make that part of your communication strategy.

BRIDGING THE GAP

Slap-Your-Head Obvious Solution

As you read this chapter, you may be thinking, "Well, duh. How could I be so stupid? Of course I need to get people involved in big changes that affect their lives." You see the problem and, not only that, you know what to do to get people engaged.

Lack of Knowledge

As Yogi Berra once said, "You've got to have deep depth." A reorganization is different from a software installation or a Lean/Six Sigma process. Learn the basics of what needs to happen. Get acquainted with the various approaches to getting started. Pay special attention to things that have worked in your own organization. Make it your job to learn from the people who got things started well. What did they do? What did they avoid? What would they do differently? What advice can they give you?

Lack of Skill

If the type of approach I discuss in this chapter is new to you, give yourself room to practice and fail. When the stakes are too high, it is very difficult to step back and learn from experience. Consider a smaller project or working with a small group on part of a change. For example, what if you were to hold a two-hour meeting (if the thought of that makes you go apoplectic, then a one-hour meeting will do), and all you did was ask people to give feedback on an idea you were considering? You could ask, "What do you like about it? What doesn't work for you? How would you suggest I change it?" And then, after everyone has gone back to his or her own offices, critique your own performance in that short meeting. It's the accumulation of these relatively small moments that builds skill. Even better, ask a trusted colleague to sit in and give you feedback.

> **TOOLKIT** For a copy of the Support for Change Questionnaire, visit www.askaboutchange.com and search for **support change questionnaire**.

Competing Beliefs

Let's say you do want to Get Started on the Right Foot, and you believe the best way to do that is to get people deeply engaged in planning and implementation. So far, so good. But as Kegan and Lahey's book *Immunity to Change* suggests, you may have some competing commitments that are *as strong* as your desire to involve others. For instance, you might be concerned that things could get out of control—or more precisely—you could lose control. So, quite unconsciously, you make a commitment to ensure that everything goes according to plan. You design a tight agenda with lots of scripted presentations. You control the amount of time given to questions and answers. You leave no room for chaos or conflict.

A key to bridging the gap is identifying ways in which you may be pulled in two directions. Chapter 11, "Moving Toward Mastery," covers several ways of working with these conflicting goals.

Context

If you work in an organization that has a history of high employee and middle management involvement, you will probably have an easier time suggesting approaches that get lots of people together to collectively roll up their sleeves to get things done. However, if you work in an organization where this type of employee involvement is countercultural, you may have to start small. You may need to demonstrate that what you are doing actually works well. You might try getting people involved to help you plan a portion of a change. Or choose a project where the eyes of corporate are not on every move you make.

HOW YOU KNOW YOU'VE STARTED ON THE RIGHT FOOT

In ballroom dancing, when you start off with the wrong foot, the dancers are off balance and the struggle to get back in sync is obvious. In the same way, there are clear signals that everyone who needs to be involved in the process is engaged in a coordinated effort.

Vision. You created a vision or goal statement that is clear. Anyone who looks at it should know where your organization is headed. Ask a stranger what your vision statement means. If they start mumbling vague comments about growth and opportunity and customer service, you're not there yet.

A plan is in place. Since there are many different types of change you could be leading, from highly technical to marketing to human resources, it is important that your plan addresses the issues critical for that type of initiative. The plan must include

- the vision or goals
- benchmarks
- timelines
- assignments (Everyone knows what is expected of him or her. And every unit knows what is expected of it as well.)
- deadlines that everyone knows
- a way to monitor progress and self-correct

Understand Direction. Everyone who is involved in planning this change needs to know

- why a change is needed (Making a Compelling Case)
- where it's headed (Results)
- what's involved in the plan (Getting Started)
- and timelines and end date (Keeping Change Alive)

Communicate with Others. The planners should be able to articulate to anyone who asks those four items defining the direction you are taking. Messy communication will lead to messy understanding by people in your organization. Try this out. Randomly ask people on your team, "Where are we headed? Why? How will we know if we've accomplished what we set out to do?"

Troubleshooting Resources in Place. People need a place to call when things start to go off course or if they just need clarity. It may be a help center, the head of the implementation team, or Mary Ann. This resource doesn't have to be an official function listed on an organization chart, but it does need to be a real resource. You call, things get done.

Everyone Knows Who Owns This Change. It's nice to say we are all in it together and we work collaboratively, but somebody has got to be in charge. They can serve at the behest of the collective if you like, but committees lack clarity and muscle. You need someone who is empowered to make decisions on the spot when needed.

You've Built the Support You Need with Supervisors. These are the people (or the person) who need to support you when there is pressure to divert attention from the project. They go to bat for your budget. Provide access to other key players. It is way too easy to forget about them in all the excitement of starting something new.

Once you get things started, you need to start putting the new systems in place. That leads us to the next chapter, "How to Keep Change Alive."

The Power of Getting People Talking About the Things They Care About

An Interview with Carolyn Lukensmeyer

*Carolyn Lukensmeyer is the founder of America*Speaks. *Prior to that she was chief of staff to the Governor of Ohio, consultant to the White House chief of staff, and deputy project director for Management for National Performance Review, more popularly known as Reinventing Government (www.americaspeaks.org).*

RM: Tell me a bit about America*Speaks*.

CL: I founded America*Speaks* in 1995 because of my deep concern about the health of democracy in the U.S. If you fastforward to where we are today, the issues about how dysfunctional our democracy is are writ large on the public stage.

We know that the vast majority of Americans in the country want significant change on the big issues: health care, immigration, budget deficits. But given the way partisan and electoral politics work, once members of Congress are seated on the Hill, they no longer reflect the country in terms of the vast middle whose interest and energy is focused on solving problems.

The good news about the American public is that when we are collectively discussing our issues together, the vast majority of us still feel responsible for the whole. The question leads directly into what your book is about: if we know that people have the impulse to want to contribute good to the whole, then the challenge becomes what kinds of processes, mechanisms, and structures do we set up that are palpable and real to people so that their voice is actually influencing not just their personal world, but has a connection to the big picture.

That is the essence of America*Speaks*' work. We relink the ordinary public to the people they have chosen as their elected officials who are making public policy decisions.

RM: How can this level of "citizen" involvement be applied inside organizations on large transformational changes?

CL: There are three very basic things leaders must address in order for a broad scale participatory change strategy to work.

First, they must actually believe in it.

Second, many of these kinds of strategies, both in the public sector and private sector, never do a sufficiently comprehensive analysis of the context. They fail to bring into the strategy all of the threads—data, options for action, and practical considerations, etc. And it is bereft of a sufficient grounding in the reality of the various different hierarchal levels and different functional perspectives. You need all of these to achieve transformative change.

Third, the leader needs to make a fundamental decision about inclusion/exclusion. It is a big leap for most organizations and many communities to open up this kind of strategic decision making to involve many, many players who traditionally would not have been involved by virtue of their numbers or their place in the hierarchy.

Leaders' sense of protecting their own interests often leads them to make premature or erroneous decisions about how wide to cast the net in the development of strategy.

RM: Failing to cast a wide net seems to be a very big problem.

CL: This problem is even more evident inside large corporate organizations or government organizations than it is when you are dealing with the public. The phenomenon of status optimism, the more power I have, the more information that comes to me without even having to ask for it, the more likely I am to be optimistic about our ability to create this change without a lot of input.

Very often, the key people who are creating the strategy, and I think consultants are as culpable of this as managers are, are overinfluenced by the status optimism of people at the top. Therefore, they make strategic errors about what kind of information they need and who they need to hear from.

RM: I've heard you say that we tend to overpolarize good and bad, who is right and who is wrong, and so forth. Why do you think that occurs?

CL: There are many reasons. One is how the human brain works. We like to categorize things. We like to differentiate. We go through our life having a set of experiences which then translate either into an accurate perception or stereotype, depending upon how they are applied. So we tend to take our own categories as more prima facie evidence than small bits of new data that would challenge our assumptions.

If we are really going to do transformative change, those are exactly the kinds of boundaries that have to be destructured. Even if I believe in this transformative change, when you start destructuring my function, I am going to resist, unless—and this is why the participation is so critical—unless I have been brought into the process early enough and deep enough so that I am actually part of the discovery process that is determining that my function has to be destructured.

This is why it is so significant for us to get more and more sophisticated about the iterative use of small- and large-scale participation processes. At a certain stage you don't always have to jump to a large-scale intervention, but in the dynamic I was just describing, the larger you go earlier in the process, the more people whose jobs are going to be directly impacted have been at the table sharing in the analysis that leads them to understand why their jobs are going to be impacted.

RM: Sometimes this deep involvement is limited to one point in the life of a change. I think this is dangerous.

CL: I agree. Management gets what they want and everybody goes back to business as usual in terms of those voices in the governing process of the organization. And there is no excuse for not figuring out information and communication resources—face to face, electronic, and so on—that bring in the employee voices or lower-level manager voices or whoever it is that needs to be involved in a systematic, ongoing way.

8

How to Keep Change Alive

The most radical revolutionary will become a conservative the day after the revolution.

—Hannah Arendt

The CEO of a large firm flew from New York to a conference in the Southwest just to deliver the opening comments to a team that was working on an important project. He could have set up a video conference link or sent a senior person to express his best wishes, but he didn't. He knew that the words wouldn't matter much. He spent a day on a plane to get there and a day to get home, because he knew that his presence sent a signal to everyone in the room (and around the firm) that this was an important endeavor to him personally.

Keeping Change Alive is a tough stage in the life of a major change. Whatever excitement people felt during the early stages of exploring options and setting direction is often long gone. Projects that had lots of resources—money, key players, and good minds to think about strategy in the early stages—sometimes find that it is hard to keep enthusiasm going. Resources dry up and the project dies.

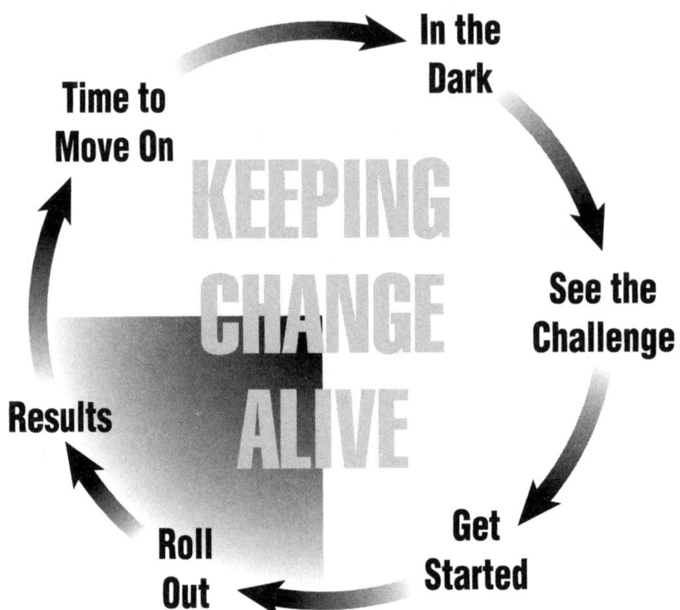

You are looking for results. But this is also the time when consulting contracts end. Many such contracts end at Roll Out on the cycle. At first glance, that seems to make sense. They helped you analyze the current state and develop a comprehensive plan. They convened planning meetings and provided expert resources. They offered training and installed new systems. You'd think that'd be enough, but it isn't. All you do at Roll Out is tell the organization, "Today, we go live." Real benefits don't come rolling in until you get to the Results stage. And that takes a lot more effort.

Take it from Miles Cook, who writes in *Pulling Away: Managing and Sustaining Change*, "In one survey, executives reported that their average cost reduction project only returned 56 percent of the estimated savings, a pretty disappointing statistic. Most executives say that the savings estimates upfront were fine. They blame the gap on a failure to execute the required changes."[1]

WHAT DOES IT MEAN TO KEEP CHANGE ALIVE?

There are three things that need to happen to Keep Change Alive. First, you must make sure that all systems, procedures, and new ways of working are implemented. Second, you need to monitor this roll out to make sure that all this effort leads you to results. Finally, you must sustain these improvements over time. Old corporate habits die hard, and everyone needs reminders and reinforcement so that focus remains on continuing to get the benefits you need from this change.

Levels 1, 2, and 3 are just as important during this stage as in all the others, but they tend to get taken for granted this far along in the life of a change.

> **Level 1:** People need information to do their jobs. This includes access to measurements and the numbers that drive their part of the business.
>
> **Level 2:** People need to continue to feel the urgency of this change. If you are not careful, people will lose their emotional momentum. When that happens, people's attention goes elsewhere and there is a risk that important tasks will get ignored or completed in a mindless fashion.
>
> **Level 3:** People need to know that you are still 100 percent committed to this project (more about this later in the chapter).

The three levels are especially worthy of your attention because it's likely that new people are coming onto the project and old people are transferring out. You've got to treat each of these shifts in personnel as an opportunity to make a compelling case, give them a history of the project to date, and let them know precisely what's expected of them today. Vague generalities won't do.

THINGS TO AVOID

Taking the Tasks for Granted

What it takes to Keep Change Alive is a long list of pretty routine and not-all-that-sexy tasks. They almost seem too mundane for a real leader to have to pay attention to. They are pedestrian tasks. They aren't a lot of fun to monitor. Success on any one of these isn't likely to earn you standing ovations at the next corporate retreat. And yet these tasks are the very things that will support movement from Getting Started to Roll Out to Results.

My Suggestion: If you are good at attending to detail, then now's the time. If not, delegate this to someone who is good at it and is excited about making sure this project is a success. Give this person your full support. Tell him or her that your door is always open, and mean it. Check in frequently. It can be a tough job and one in which people often get little recognition for their work. Don't let that happen.

Delegating Enthusiasm

You can't delegate enthusiasm. You can try to create a cadre of people who are as excited as you, but in the end, people need to know that *you* are 100 percent behind this project. They must believe that this project remains a high priority for you—and see proof that you are still a champion for its successful implementation.

The people who need to support you are very busy (just like you are). If they see signs that this change is no longer one of your top three projects, their attention will turn quickly to other projects that they believe are more important. Remember, they've got Cycles of Change already working on other projects, and your lack of commitment is an opportunity for them to get back to "important" work.

My Suggestion: Every Monday morning (or whenever you do your weekly calendar) make sure that you find places to reinforce how important this project is to you. You are at a critical stage in the life of this change. Don't let this task slide.

Keeping a Project Alive That Should Have Died

Not every project should make it around the cycle. When you pick up those strong signs, have the courage to pull the plug.

For example:

- Your customers demand something else. It's often been said that IBM stayed with mainframe computers way too long and missed the early wave of personal computing. True enough. But when they finally believed this shift was taking place, they did a masterful job of entering the PC market.
- Demographics shifted and you've got a new customer base who isn't terribly interested in the products you've got in the pipeline. I have been impressed by the response of large urban libraries that have experienced major demographic shifts. They have found ways to make the library enticing to younger people by keeping up with technology and making these public institutions more appealing to people from different cultures. Even our branch

libraries here in Arlington, Virginia, have Internet connections for patrons. Books are now surrounded by other media such as DVDs and CDs. Librarians reach out to new communities. I've heard that in our relatively small county of about 150,000 people, there are over 100 languages spoken.

- New threats cause you to shift your focus. Once security agencies realized that threats could come from anywhere, not just nations, they examined their priorities and made shifts in where they focused their attention.

And the list goes on.

My Suggestion: Invite opinions that differ from yours so that you can hear about changing conditions from people who may be closer to your customers. If everyone always agrees with you, don't congratulate yourself on your perfection. Assume that people can't tell you what they think. You just can't be that perfect, in spite of what your mom always told you.

(And make sure you keep your antennae alert to changes in your overall environment.)

Forgetting to Remind People About the Need to Make a Compelling Case for Change

A sense of urgency doesn't last forever. What got our attention eighteen months ago may have dissipated. It is important to pay attention to these signals that let you know if people still feel a compelling need for a change or not. If they don't feel the urgency, then it is time to review chapter 6, "How to Make a Compelling Case for Change," and focus on addressing the Level 1, 2, and 3 issues that get people's attention.

Also remember that some employees have left teams and others have joined over the course of this project. You can't expect these new people to magically feel the urgency. Before giving them a playbook, make sure they see and feel why this change is so desperately needed.

TOOLKIT For a printable checklist of these Keeping Change Alive items, visit www.askaboutchange.com and search for **change alive checklist**.

My Suggestion: Put this task on your calendar or delegate it to someone else. Let him know that making sure urgency stays high is critically important. As with any delegation, be available to this person.

WHAT IT TAKES TO KEEP CHANGE ALIVE

Keeping energy high during a major change can be challenging. It is all too common for people to be excited about a new initiative, only to see that interest wane over the coming months. There are no easy answers or quick-fix solutions. However, the following things need to be in place if you want to move an organization from In the Dark to Results.

As the leader of this change, think about "what it takes" with regard to what you need to do personally and what you need to make sure gets done.

What You Need to Do Personally

You Must Be the Champion for This Change

Although I was never a fan of reengineering in the way that it was commonly implemented, one idea from Michael Hammer and James Champy[2] made good sense. They suggest that you need a czar to lead the change. This person is given the authority and resources to make this change a reality. This person needs to have clout in the organization. He or she need not be a senior manger, but must be an influential player. It can't be someone who happens to be between projects or isn't valuable enough to do "real work."

Let's assume you are that person. In order to be a real champion or "czar". . .

You Need a Clear Contract

The czar needs a clear contract with whomever he or she reports to. You need to know what support you can expect from your sponsors. What will they do when the unexpected happens? What help can you expect from them throughout the life of the project? It's crucial that you are able to talk to them about these issues. You need to know that they've got your back.

It's critical to your success that your sponsors enter this agreement with their eyes open. They've got to be able to see the potential pitfalls of the project. If they only get goo-goo eyed over possibilities but fail to see the inherent risks, you are putting yourself in a vulnerable position. As athletes and investors say, they need to have skin in the game too.

Check out the "Contract with Other Leaders" section later in this chapter. In addition to using it with people you delegate to, I recommend that you try it as a framework for the conversation with your sponsor.

A champion needs to be out there. People need to know that you are 100 percent committed to the success of this project. If it means getting on a plane to kick off a meeting, you're there. If it means that you need to run interference when other leaders try to steal talent or budget, you've got to act.

You've got to keep this change on the agenda. It can never fall below the top few items that are always talked about. Even if the only thing you ask at a weekly staff meeting is, "Kathy, Bill, Chris, where do things stand with the project?" it lets people know that this change is still important to you.

It would be hard to overestimate the importance of people knowing that you are the champion.

Allow Yourself to Be Influenced

Lots of unintended things can happen in the life of a change. Pay attention and be open to information that you might not want to hear.

You desperately need people who aren't afraid to tell you the truth as they see it. Cultivate these relationships because these people could keep you out of trouble. A vice-president in a company has junior weather forecasters around the organization to give her timely weather reports. These people act like the volunteers who provide weather forecasts from their backyard to supplement the meteorologist's predictions on the evening news. They do not act like the Stasi and name names. Their role is informal and this lets the leader know how people are reacting to changes.

Attend to Power and Politics

All organizations are political. Good leaders know this and they know how things get done. You might review the items listed under Theory X and Theory Y in chapter 5, "Ignore the Context at Your Peril." If you can't change the culture, then you do need to make it safe for people to work on this project so they don't put their careers in jeopardy.

Betty was a leader of a small team in a large nonprofit. The head boss was generally feared. He had a habit of micromanaging to the extent of going into people's word processor documents and changing text during the night. There were a lot of "yes people" and sycophants in that office because groveling was a good way to keep your job. But groveling wasn't a good way to get exceptional work accomplished, something Betty was able to do. She surrounded herself with a magnificent team who combined talent and commitment to good work. Her unit was very successful.

Often I imagined her holding a large umbrella over the staff during a hurricane. She kept her staff safe, but she took some hits from all that rain and wind. I believe that because her team did such good work (and brought in lots of money for the organization), she remained standing in spite of being bruised.

Protect the Process

In other words, beware of "scope creep." Many projects move beyond their original scope. Like bills before the legislature, these initiatives get weighed down by all types of extraneous related and unrelated projects. As the leader, you need to protect the project team and anyone else who is working to make this project a success.

When Deloitte & Touche was implementing its highly regarded Women's Initiative (an effort to keep talented women working at their firm), someone suggested that the team take on other issues of diversity since they were doing such a good job. Someone else wisely said no. The firm could learn from how they built support for the Women's Initiative, and then create a new team to work on other diversity issues. The extra baggage could have created too much of a burden on that highly effective team.

Unless the situation changes dramatically, stick to the original plan. And if you need to deviate from the original plan, do it consciously. Reexamine resources, assignments to the project, and so forth. Plan for the unexpected today. Determine what you will do if the scope begins to change or if conditions change.

What You Need to Make Sure Gets Done

As czar, there are some things you need to make sure get done. Please don't let that title go to your head. Remind yourself about the history of the Romanovs, just to keep things in perspective. You may need to use your power, but do it in a way that doesn't get you exiled to Siberia.

You may want to take responsibility for some of the following tasks, but these are things that can be easily delegated provided you have a clear contract with the people who report to you.

Symbolic Acts

When Continental Airlines made it on the list as one of the top five airlines, CEO Gordon Bethune sent everyone in the company a check for $65. OK, that's not a lot of money, but it went to everyone. And everyone got the same amount.

Be careful here. Giving $65 to everyone was a symbolic act. No one could have confused it with compensation. It was a way of saying thank you.

In *Sway,* Ori Brafman and Rom Brafman argue that offering actual compensation can backfire. They write about how the Swiss government tried to induce the residents of two small towns to allow the government to build nuclear waste dumps in their backyards. The government started to offer financial incentives. To everyone's surprise, "the percentage of people who said they would accept the proposition not only didn't increase—it *fell* by half."[3] They report other studies where compensation is offered as incentive and performance actually dropped.

Work at an Appropriate Speed

Determine how fast you can move on this project and still get the level of commitment you need. Sometimes perfectly fine changes die simply because the organization moved too slowly. Everyone does not have to be trained. All systems don't have to be in place. Find ways to get to Roll Out.

Back in the day when quality was all the rage, many organizations failed simply because they moved too slowly. They were never able to build momentum or a sense of urgency. Things proceeded at such a slow incremental pace that early adopters lost steam before others were on board.

Ownership

Make certain that there is sufficient ownership for this new initiative. Ask yourself, "Do enough people support this initiative for it to make it from Getting Started through to Results?" If the answer is no, you need to spend more time helping people to See the Challenge on the Cycle of Change and make sure the Getting Started steps were addressed adequately.

Resources

Are adequate resources committed to ensuring implementation? Resources might include sufficient budget, time for training, and other people. A critical resource is time and attention. Can the leaders of this change dedicate sufficient time to make it work? If this is a major change and you ask people to work on it along with all the other tasks they've been doing, you can expect the change to fail.

Rewards

Will people be rewarded for this work? Will people get credit for this project? In other words, will this be considered a major objective on their performance plans? Will opportunities for good assignments and promotions be available to the people who work on this, or will this project be a corporate wasteland?

Making Sure Delegation Works

Early in the life of a major change you will need to delegate portions of the initiative to various individuals, teams, and departments. The handoff from you to them is critically important. If you fumble or if they fail to pick up the ball, everything is at risk.

Contract with Other Leaders

If you are the leader of a major change, you will probably need to delegate large portions of the project. There is a big difference between dumping something on someone's desk and actually delegating. I encourage you to hold conversations with each of these leaders. (And you might consider asking your sponsor to talk with you about these critical themes.)[4]

Here are some tips for delegating responsibility effectively. First, three things need to be in place in order for you to delegate effectively.

1. **They need to understand what this change is all about.** Why now? Why this change? In other words, let them know "why" and "what" before you get into "how" to do it. The middle managers who will be leading portions of the change need context in order to make good decisions. Without that understanding, they have to make it up as they go along—guessing why this is important and trying to intuit what's most important every step of the way. Why leave this to chance? Explain what's going on.
2. **They need to understand what's at stake.** What's driving this change—new competition, the need to respond quicker to challenges in your environment, fear that great performance today may not equal great performance in the coming years? What's the risk if you fail? What's the risk if you do nothing?
3. **They need to trust you (and other senior managers).** If they don't think you will see this through, they will probably do just enough work to keep you off their backs until you turn your attention to something else. You need to demonstrate that you are a capable leader. In other words, you plan to oversee this

project from beginning to end. You will fight for resources. You will not be distracted by other new priorities.

Once these things are in place, then you can start handing off. Below are things to include in your contracting conversation with those you plan to delegate or assign tasks to.

Create a Contract

A very good way to hand off the assignment is to develop a simple contract with the leaders who will be assigned to plan and carry out various parts of the change. This contract should include:

Common Understanding of Outcome

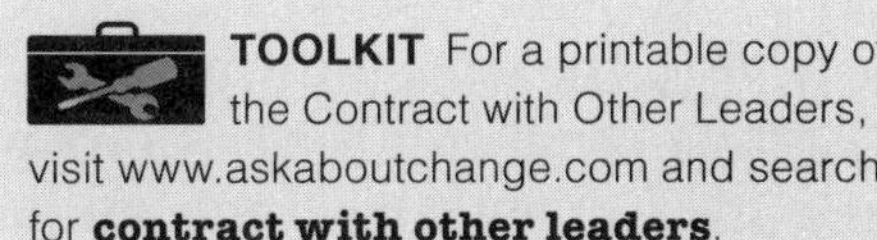

TOOLKIT For a printable copy of the Contract with Other Leaders, visit www.askaboutchange.com and search for **contract with other leaders**.

Make sure that you and the people or groups you delegate to have a common understanding of what is expected. Explain your picture of success. What does it look like? How will you know when you are successful? Remember Robert Mager's advice about goals and objectives: if you met that goal on the street, you'd recognize it.

Specific Milestones and Completion Date

Explain how they will be able to measure success along the way. What are the metrics you will use? If you don't have a good answer for this question, then turn to the people you are delegating to and develop clear, measurable milestones in collaboration with them.

Let people know how much detail you will need as they go along. Some leaders want to be in the loop every step of the way. Others prefer minimal updates. Make sure the people you are delegating to know what you want.

Resources

Ask what they will need in order to meet these targets. For example:

- **People.** Who do they need in order to be successful? Perhaps they will want access to an engineer in another location or a marketing whiz from across the country.
- **Money.** What's the budget for their portion of the project?

- **Access to other stakeholders.** Ask who else they will need to be able to talk to in order to be successful. Often these will be your peers. And you can be the link that opens those doors.
- **Access to you.** Discuss the best ways for you to stay in touch. And tell them the best way to contact you when they have an urgent question.
- **Time.** These people are probably already overworked. You can't just add another major project and expect it will get done. You've got to be willing to readjust priorities. If you don't, then you risk seeing a lot of projects either die or come in well below expectations.

Anticipate Glitches

With the help of the people you are delegating to, brainstorm things that could go wrong. (Don't pretend that this time will be different than all the others. Plan for the unexpected.)

Identify those glitches that are important to address today. Discuss what you can do to protect against those things happening. What are the early warning signs that a glitch might be about to occur? What contingency plans will you put in place to avert a major problem?

Review

Make sure that everyone is clear about all parts of this contract. Thank people for coming—and then get started. This simple process gets major changes off on the right foot and can save you many headaches, busted reputations, and potential failures.

BUILDING CAPACITY FOR THE NEXT TIME AND THE TIME AFTER THAT

I find it stunning how many changes succeed or fail with little or no thoughtful analysis of what occurred. The U.S. Department of Defense developed After Action Reports as a way to debrief any important event. This approach has found its way into some other government agencies as well as some corporations. It is now commonly referred to by the acronym—AAR. (Remember, the government thought it up so it has to have an acronym.) Some would say that Julius Caesar's *Commentaries on the Gallic War* was the first recorded instance of a thoughtful AAR.

TOOLKIT For an AAR discussion tool, visit www.askaboutchange.com and search for **AAR discussion tool**.

The AAR

The After Action Report (AAR) can help you begin to see patterns—things you want to keep in the act and things you want to avoid doing next time. It is a tool that will allow you to build your capacity to lead change.

The process itself is quite simple—all it takes is courage. You have to be willing to hear the truth. And that's not always easy. If a major project dies before ever achieving any measurable results, the temptation often is to let the change die quietly. Others are usually happy to collude with you on this, and soon the project fades from anyone's attention. Reputations are saved, but no one learns from the experience.

An AAR usually covers a few fundamental questions:

- What were our goals or expectations?
- What worked well?
- What didn't?
- What did we learn?
- What will we do differently in the future?

If you do a Google search on "after action reports" you will find templates and examples of completed AARs.

Why an After Action Report Might Fail

I do see a big risk in filling out an AAR. The completion of an After Action Report could put too much emphasis on the report itself and miss the reasons why you chose to evaluate how you did in the first place. The value of an AAR is to learn something. Reports, while sometimes necessary, take you and other major players away from the experience of reliving the events and candidly identifying pluses, minuses, and things to change next time.

Here is where your leadership needs to come into play. You need to insist that the AAR is a process fueled by dialogue among key stakeholders. And you need to be a major player in this process. You should not delegate this to anyone.

THE POSSIBILIY OF AN ORGANIZATION WHERE CAPACITY FOR CHANGE IS A GIVEN

This book is not a book about culture change as such. Its purpose is to support you so that you can lead change successfully within the current culture of your organization. Of course, you may find that you need to get the organization to move closer to Theory Y in order to get people involved in the way you like. As important as that is, it is only a part of culture change. Nevertheless, it is worth spending a few sentences whetting your appetite for how you might build a capacity to handle change differently into your unique organization.

If your corporate culture is based on Theory X (see chapter 5, "Ignore the Context at Your Peril") where there is a lack of trust in the people who do the work, then don't even try. You'll die young. Find a place where what you value has a chance of succeeding. If your current culture leans toward Theory Y, a belief in people's intrinsic motivation and desire to work, but it just lacks the know-how to embed effective change management practices into your culture, then it might be fruitful to explore ways to build the organization's capacity to handle change well.

In Jim Collins' fine book, *Good to Great,* he writes that the great companies ". . . paid scant attention to managing change, motivating people or creating alignment. Under the right conditions, the problems of commitment, alignment, motivation, and change largely melt away." They melt away!

He goes on to say, "The good-to-great companies had no name, tag line, launch event, or program to signify their transformations. Indeed, some reported being unaware of the magnitude of the transformation at the time; only later, in retrospect, did it become clear."[5]

When I first read those two paragraphs back in 2001, I was afraid organizations would give up attempts to lead change since Collins said the best ones didn't worry about such things. I worried too much. Because so few organizations ever try to implement what they read in books, it hasn't become a problem.

I don't think Collins was saying, "Don't try to lead change," but that the great companies had created cultures where the change management process itself wasn't as necessary.

I believe the key to making this transition lies, in large part, at the Making a Compelling Case for Change stage. The great companies don't need to worry about making a case because that's what they do every day. Everyone knows the important stuff about the business—strengths,

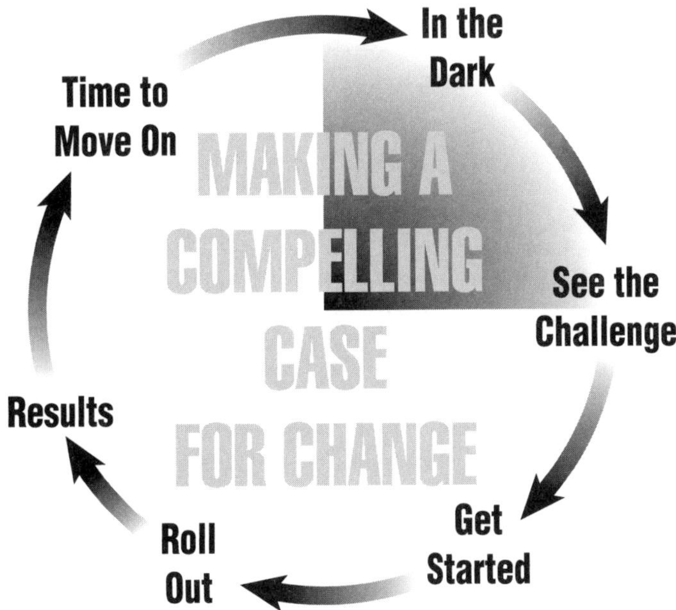

weaknesses, opportunities, and threats. People know the numbers that drive the business. They know how their contribution helps the company meet that number. So when a new enterprise-wide software system is needed, there is little push back since people can see why it is necessary. In smaller organizations that use open book management practices, the companies literally open the books and people are more fully engaged in making decisions that affect the health of the organization. (Of course, this is possible in large organizations, but it is more difficult to communicate up and down when there are many layers and locations spread across continents.)

TOOLKIT For 23 Ideas to Keep Change Alive, visit www.askaboutchange.com and search for **23 ideas**.

An organization's ability to consistently make a case requires a strong belief in people. The organization needs to believe that the employees, professional staff, and managers have what it takes to do the job and that those people are fully committed to doing the right thing. That's a Theory Y organization in my book.

When I work in organizations, I am always interested in the extent to which people know what's going on and the extent to which they have a say in the future of the business. That information tells me a lot about the organization's mindset, its real set of values (not those things posted on the wall). If I were going to try to change a culture so that it was more responsive to the type of change management we are exploring in this book, I'd start by looking at what gets in the way of making a compelling case for change.

BRIDGING THE GAP

Slap-Your-Head Obvious Solution

With any luck, when you read the section "What It Takes to Keep Change Alive," you saw some of the big things that help keep change alive and realized that you could easily make sure those things get done. But this stage of a change, more than any other, lends itself to thinking that we will do better than we actually do. The solutions to keeping things moving ahead are so obvious that it is easy to take them for granted.

Lack of Knowledge

If you have any lack of knowledge in this stage, I imagine that it's subtle. You may wonder what the signals are that let you know that you are "moving at an appropriate speed" or understand the demands of effective delegation. This is a great place to pay close attention to others in your organization who handle this stage well. They will show you how it's done in the unique political and cultural environment where you both work. Ask them how they would handle a real-life or hypothetical change project at this stage, or invite their advice on the situation you are currently in.

Lack of Skill

In *The Checklist Manifesto,*[6] Atul Gawande writes that surgeons who use checklists perform better, safer surgeries. Flight crews who follow the proscribed checklists don't have to worry about forgetting some small but important task. I urge you to consider using a checklist as well. Unless you are adept at implementing the skills it takes to keep change alive, consider the lowly checklist. The items covered in this chapter are easy to agree with and pretty easy to overlook.

Competing Beliefs and Context

I'm going out on a limb here, but as a leader, you are probably interested in seeing the projects you lead actually achieve the intended results. However, there probably are competing interests that pull you away from that goal.

Some of those pulls may come from you personally. You want to make sure you keep your eyes on the horizon, on the lookout for new opportunities and possible threats. Consequently, you believe that attending to the minutia of keeping change alive will divert you from the tasks "real" leaders perform.

TOOLKIT For a podcast interview with J. R. McGee on ways to sustain commitment to change, visit www.askaboutchange.com and search for **sustain change**.

Your organization may put demands on you that cause you to take your eyes off the goal of leading a particular new project to completion. For instance, the organization may demand that you spend 80 percent of your time on the road in wildly different time zones. Or you might be rewarded for starting new things and punished for sticking with a change from beginning to end.

I hope you can see how your personal goals can be influenced by the context you work in. And these competing forces can make it difficult to be clear about what you really want and how you will set priorities that you think are best.

HOW TO TELL WHEN YOU'VE SUCCEEDED IN KEEPING CHANGE ALIVE

Reflect on other changes in your organization and identify what distinguished those that succeeded. Learn from the things your colleagues have done. That way you can spot the signals that your work is succeeding. In other words, take the AAR (After Action Report) process seriously. You can learn a lot by taking a sober look at past successes and failures.

There are systems in place to support this change. These systems could include:

- Communication processes that ensure people are able to get the information they need when they need it and provide timely data, concerns, and questions to others
- Ways of monitoring progress so that you can catch glitches and other problems quickly
- Reporting structures that support the new program
- A performance management system that focuses on completion of goals related to this new initiative. Too often, people are asked to work hard on a new project but realize that at the end of the year their performance will be judged using other criteria

- IT platforms and software, and people using new approaches for improving quality and service.

Remember, the purpose of Keep Change Alive activities is to get to Results on the cycle. So once systems are in place, then it's time to see if you are getting the results you wanted. People received the training they need. The new program or project was launched successfully. You learned from pilot tests and the initial launch and have improved the process so that it is running as you had hoped it would.

It may take a while (perhaps a long while) before the launch of a new program generates results. That's why, as the leader, you must keep the focus on this change.

9

Getting Back on Track

Ye shall know the truth, and the truth shall make you mad.

—Aldous Huxley

Five days before its massive eruption in 1980, Mount Saint Helens simmered and smoked as pressure built inside. Everyone knew it would blow, but none could predict its power. How high would flames shoot into the Washington sky? How much molten rock would vomit from its mouth—and where would the lava run? Resistance is a lot like Mount Saint Helens. You can guess, you can make estimates, but you can't tell for certain how strong it will be until it erupts. Polite conversations, hurried executive briefings, lip-service exchanges with staff give only a hint of the pressure that builds deep below the surface.

With good reason, people are frightened of volcanoes. Most residents and visitors clear off the mountain well in advance of the eruption. Getting out of the way of spewing lava makes sense, and that's why the notion of embracing resistance may seem crazy. To deal with resistance effectively you must be willing to summon its fire. You must encourage flames and red-hot ashes to shoot high into the conference room. You cannot be satisfied with whiffs of smoke; you need to feel the rumbling roar of its full force. This chapter focuses on ways to embrace resistance.

WHAT IT MEANS TO GET BACK ON TRACK

You are in the middle of a massive change and you begin to see that things have slowed down and maybe even stopped in some places. As you look around, you see that it is not a budget crisis or some emergency that has diverted people's attention—people really dislike this new initiative.

You remind people what's expected of them. That doesn't work. You threaten and punish. That doesn't work. You bring in a motivational speaker. And people laugh. What's left?

TOOLKIT For a podcast on why things get off track, visit www.askaboutchange.com and search for **back on track**.

You could try finding out why people seem to be opposing this idea (or perhaps opposing you). You can decide to embrace the resistance. Why take this counterintuitive approach? Since you cannot anticipate the extent of resistance until you see it and feel its heat, you've got to find out where it's coming from.

If you think of resistance as energy, you can see that the only way to use it productively is to let it surface. Imagine a large generator, capable of transforming fire and heat into electricity, sitting atop Mount Saint Helens. That powerful energy is available to you only when the volcano is erupting. Of course, you need to find ways to unleash that force safely.

WHAT TO AVOID

Assuming That Things Will Get Better If We Just Forge Ahead

If things start to go seriously off track, you've got to deal with it. Energy can work for you or against you. Unless the problem is lack of funds or some major technical glitch, then you are about to face massive resistance. Once the energy turns against the project, that resistance will build and build.

My Suggestion: Slow down and consider the consequences if you are wrong. At the very least, assess what's going on at Levels 1, 2, and 3. You'll see suggestions for getting at this information later in this chapter.

Playing Hardball

When people resist us, it can bring out the worst in us. A knee-jerk reaction is triggered and we take charge in a not-too-pretty manner. We threaten, demand, fire, replace people, humiliate, and then we get nasty!

My Suggestion: Reread the section on working with knee-jerk reactions in chapter 4. If you are going to emulate a tyrant, do it as a conscious decision and not as a knee-jerk reaction. There is an easy way to tell the difference. If you have considered the unintended consequences of going ballistic and you still want to use that tactic, it's probably not a knee-jerk reaction. Personally, I'd still advise against that approach. Strong tactics can backfire and create bad blood for future changes. It also sends the message that when there's a problem your first response will be to take back control from others.

Grabbing at the First Bone

Strong resistance isn't pretty. It brings out Level 2 feelings of being attacked and threatened. As a leader, you will probably find yourself trying to keep your knee-jerk reactions at bay. So, when you get something—anything—that looks like it might be the reason people are resisting, you jump on it just to ease the tension. And you go about fixing that problem. But later you learn that you fixed the wrong problem.

My Suggestion: Keep looking to make sure you've learned the real reasons why things have slowed to a halt. This won't be easy, but it will be far better than fixing an insignificant issue.

WHAT IT TAKES TO GET BACK ON TRACK

Before you can do anything else, you need to notice that people are actually resisting you.

Pick Up the Signs

Yogi Berra once said, "You can observe a lot just by watching." Once you know what to look for, you begin to see the many faces of resistance. That's the first step. Once you see it, you can address it. You might want to review the ways to spot resistance that are covered in chapter 3:

- confusion
- quick criticism

- denial and deflection
- malicious compliance
- sabotage
- easy agreement
- silence
- in-your-face criticism

You may see the silence of the resistance in a meeting, hear a strong-willed rebuttal as you wait for an elevator, or witness the effects of a saboteur. These are bits of information warning you that you are sitting atop that potential volcano.

Work with Resistance

Once you get a feeling that people are resisting, there are three things to do:

1. Assess what's going on (find out what the Level 1, 2, and 3 issues are).
2. Analyze what you just learned (interpret this information).
3. Act (do something to try to turn resistance back into support).

Step 1: Assess What's Going On

Think of it as creating a list. You need to know what the Level 1 (understanding), Level 2 (emotional reactions), and Level 3 (trust) issues are. And remember that all three levels have a positive side (support) and a potentially negative side (opposition).

You might learn that people understand the challenge and what's expected of them but are afraid of what's about to happen because they don't believe you have what it takes to lead such a big change effectively.

The following are some ways to find out what's on the list in your organization:

The Grunt

Employees at a large company were quite angry over management practices. An underground newspaper called *The Grunt* surfaced. It was cheap, put together on the sly. It was filled with invectives and took devastating swipes at management.

Management began to seek out those responsible for its publication—not to engage them in dialogue and learn about the issues, but to punish them. If management had acted with courage, they could have learned a lot from *The Grunt*—not so much from the content of the paper, but just from its very existence. The fact that people took the time and risk to write that underground newspaper said a lot about management-labor relations in that company. Unfortunately, senior management's search-and-destroy mission just added to the fear and suspicion.

The Grunt appeared back in the days of mimeographs. They had to hide the machine from prying eyes. Today, *The Grunt* might appear as a blog or in a chat room on a social networking site. Keep your eyes open for signs of *The Grunt* in your neighborhood.

Restroom Talk

The signals of resistance are sometimes difficult to see and are best picked up outside the official forums—in restrooms, on elevators, over lunch, in hallways, or while perusing your organization's version of *The Grunt.*

A few years ago I was observing a group of managers discussing the challenges and changes facing their organization. The meeting seemed to be going along well. Nothing in their words or actions indicated a problem. It wasn't until we took a break and I ran into one of the players in the men's room that I learned the truth. I asked, "How's the meeting going?" To my surprise, he said, "Same old stuff. We never get anything done." Later I ran into another manager. Her reply was similar. On and on it went—no one thought this was a productive meeting, yet when they met no one ever mentioned dissatisfaction.

TOOLKIT For an article on knowing when to keep going and when to walk away, visit www.askaboutchange.com and search for **know when to walk away.**

Solicit Feedback Before Meeting Face to Face

Listening to a roomful of people light into you and your pet ideas takes tremendous courage. And it is a very dangerous approach to try. When you hear raw, unfiltered criticism, you may respond with defensive knee-jerk reactions. I have seen people lash back at those who were speaking candidly. When you do this, you just make matters worse. Once people see that it is unsafe to speak, they quit talking. Try a safer alternative.

A division manager of a financial services company was beginning to hear mounting criticism of some changes he had initiated. Although most everyone in the organization recognized that they had to stay ahead of the competition in providing the highest quality service, they wondered whether he was serious about the changes. What impact would these changes have on careers? He asked everyone who had a concern or question to write it anonymously and submit it to him prior to an all-hands meeting. That way he could look at all the papers before he faced his 100-person management team.

In the meeting, I watched him respond openly to all the questions and comments. Because he seemed to appreciate the questions, others began asking follow-up questions from the floor. He had found a safe way to invite and unleash some of the major criticism and concern about his program. Would he hear all of it in a single meeting? Probably not. The actual eruptions on Mount Saint Helens lasted for weeks. Why should our lives be any easier? But it was a great start.

Make It Easy for People to Speak

Start with the familiar: allow people to talk with others whom they trust. During a particularly painful reorganization, senior management needed to hear what was blocking implementation. It was important for all units to get crucial issues out on the table. People began by discussing these issues in their own groups first. By starting to work in familiar surroundings, people gained comfort talking about the issues. One person recorded comments and reported the results of the discussion to the entire group. Since comments were not attributed to the individuals who made them, people felt some degree of safety.

TOOLKIT For tips on engaging in dialogue, visit www.askaboutchange.com and search for **dialogue tips**.

Once issues are mentioned publicly, the spell is lifted. People often feel free to address things openly that an hour before were taboo.

Review Formal Surveys

Anonymous employee surveys can provide a wealth of information if you use resistance as the lens to examine the results. Many companies routinely ask staff to complete one of these attitude surveys. Typically, they include questions about leadership, teamwork, planning—virtually all aspects of management and human relations. Often managers or teams throughout the organization develop strategies to raise poor scores and keep better practices on track.

In addition to interpreting the results as you normally would, consider what they are saying in light of the proposed (or recently implemented) changes.

- Has trust in management risen or fallen?
- Do people seem surprisingly confused about the direction you are going?
- Do any of the narrative comments pertain to the changes occurring in your organization?

If you see signs of resistance embedded in these results, you must search further. Suppose that confidence in senior management has fallen from 6.2 to 3.1 over the past two years. All this tells you is that the scores have dropped dramatically; you need to learn why. You will undoubtedly make assumptions about the meaning of this decline, but you can't be certain of the significance until you ask. You must combine these survey results with some other active method of unleashing resistance—for example, a variation on Workout or focus group meetings. (See the description of Workout later in this chapter.)

I am not suggesting you commission a formal survey to get at resistance. That's overkill. But if you already have that information from a recent survey, learn from it.

Informal Questionnaires

I am a fan of informal surveys. You can prepare a survey in a few minutes to get instant information regarding a change. A few well-chosen questions can give you vital information.

I have gotten good results writing a few provocative questions (I try to limit my questions to four) and sending them out over the company's email system. Email seems to get a much quicker response and a higher rate of return than traditional paper-and-pencil surveys. (If you use email, make sure that the system allows people to send messages anonymously.) And, as with the formal surveys, use the information as a foundation for further conversation.

> **TOOLKIT** For the Getting Back on Track Questionnaire, visit www.askaboutchange.com and search for **back on track questionnaire**.

I use SurveyMonkey.com to create, send, and collect survey results. It is quick, intuitive, and very easy to use. And you can try it out for free. There are other online survey resources. Just look around.

If you use surveys, consider showing people the aggregate results, no matter how gruesome. This is part of the unleashing process. Posting the results (minus names, of course) lets everyone see how the group views

GETTING THINGS UP ON THE TABLE

Here is a process for beginning to learn about issues that might otherwise remain hidden.

1. *Assemble a group that represents a cross section of the organization—all levels and all interests. The size of the group is less important than making certain that the gathering is a microcosm of the whole.*
2. *Have people meet in their own departments (without their bosses) to discuss the items listed in the questionnaire included in the online resources. Groups rate each item and discuss reasons for their responses. Each group posts its responses on flip-chart pads. (Senior managers should form their own groups to respond to these items.)*
3. *Working on one item at a time, have each group discuss the ranking it gave and the reasons for this score. Although no critiques are allowed, encourage questions to clarify responses.*
4. *Ask everyone to help you identify points where scores are similar and places where scores are different.*
5. *Ask for reactions throughout the meeting. Be generous in giving your reactions. If you are surprised, say so. If their responses confirm your fantasies, tell them. If you are reassured by their high scores, let them know that as well.*
6. *Don't make promises on the spot, but let people know what you plan to do with what you've learned. Make sure you stick to this promise and get back to them with answers or responses.*

the change. All can look at the major issues reinforcing or inhibiting the change. People see whether they are alone in their opposition or support of the idea. Are others frightened or ecstatic? Are they asking the same questions? Survey results give everyone the same picture of reality.

If you decide to share the results, wait until you've done Step 2 (above) and analyzed the results. Then as part of Step 3, you can reveal the results, your interpretation of them, and what you plan to do differently.

I realize that sometimes there are legal issues that keep you from sharing data openly. But I have also seen leaders hide behind the "legal won't allow it" defense just so they wouldn't have to lose face in public.

Focus Groups

I like to form focus groups of about six to ten people. They meet one time for about an hour. The purpose is to gather information: What works? What doesn't?

Safety is key. People need to feel free to talk. Whoever facilitates the conversation needs to listen and paraphrase—and not react. This is no place to get on your podium and sing the virtues of your idea. Your goal is to learn.

I like to go into focus group meetings with a few key questions and then allow what I hear to influence what I ask next. I find that if I am too prepared, with too many questions, I focus more on getting everything covered than on listening and responding to what people are saying.

What Questions Do I Ask?

Whether it's a one-on-one conversation, a survey, or a focus group, I often ask four questions using the three levels as my guide.

1. To what extent do you understand what's involved in this change? (Level 1) Please explain.
2. What's your reaction to this change? (Level 2) Please explain.
3. To what extent do you trust the senior management team to lead this change effectively? (Level 3) Please explain.
4. What else?

That's it. If I am meeting face to face, then I ask follow-up questions because I want to get the clearest picture I can of what they are thinking and feeling.

Stay Focused

However you decide to gather information, stay focused on that single goal. You are there to learn what the Level 1, 2, and 3 issues are. Period.

As one of my clients told me, "The Executive Director and I went on a listening tour." I love the clarity of their intention. We are there to listen, not to preach, convince, cajole, but to just listen and learn.

And keep it simple. Ask a few questions. You may have twenty-five questions just waiting to be asked. Don't do it. When I send informal surveys and tell people that I am going to ask them four questions and it will take them five minutes or less to complete the survey, the response rate is often well over 60 percent. But when I have sent longer surveys, not only does the response rate go down, but the quality of the responses does as well. For example: What's your reaction to these changes? Answer: They're OK. What do you think of the leaders? Answer: I don't know.

When Meeting Face to Face

Here are some principles that might make it easier to meet in person with another individual or group.

Meet Privately at First. In most of the examples, people worked alone or in small groups before going public with their comments. Find a way to let people think before they speak. Most often they will give you a more thoughtful and considered response. Meeting privately often makes it easier on you as well. You are less likely to feel a need to defend your ideas or reputation.

Make It Safe to Speak. In some organizations, focus groups would not work because trust is so low. In others, people feel free to talk at any time. It is important to pick strategies that fit the organization. If you choose wrongly, you'll know. If you hold a Workout and no one comes or few speak, you may have picked the wrong approach for that group at that time.

Meet Behind Closed Doors. In the historic 1994 summit between the United States and Russia, Presidents Clinton and Yeltsin decided to hold a part of their talks behind closed doors, without the usual large groups of aides.[1] Meetings like these let people speak much more freely without fear that their com-

WORKOUT

GE's approach to getting issues out on the table and dealing with them is quite simple in design. Its power comes from the safety it offers participants.

People get away from the office or plant and dress casually. The informality and the change of location send a message that this meeting will not be business as usual.

Bosses are kept out of the room during discussions. Facilitators meet with staff to identify issues and make concrete proposals. Often people spend much of the time complaining. This unleashes the resistance and is usually followed by solid ideas.

When managers return, they must make decisions about the proposals publicly and on the spot. Typically 80 percent get immediate yes or no decisions from managers and decisions must be made on the rest within a month.

ments will be leaked out. They can speak off the record. They can disagree in private. And neither player needs to put on a good face for the audience.

Wise employees first introduce new ideas to their bosses privately. It's easier to explore objections openly away from the crowd. In a public forum, some bosses feel the need to appear aloof and authoritative, never admitting weakness or discussing options.

Remember That People Resist for Good Reasons. From their point of view, people resist your ideas for good reasons. You should keep this in mind as you inquire about their resistance. Don't zing them—just try to learn more about what's on their minds.

Don't Penalize the Truth. This links directly to the previous point. Be grateful for honesty; don't kill the messenger.

Give Yourself Time to Think. Written comments and survey results give you time to chew and digest before facing those who might oppose or question your idea.

Give Them a Target. The clearer your vision, the stronger the reaction you can expect—and that's a good thing. Ask for what you want. If you're thinking about a restructuring that will close five plants and lay off hundreds, you must tell them.

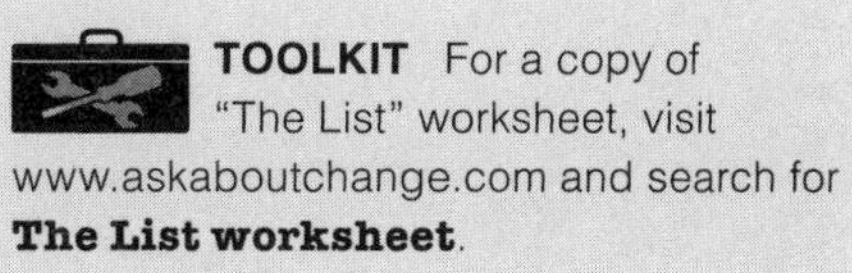
TOOLKIT For a copy of "The List" worksheet, visit www.askaboutchange.com and search for **The List worksheet**.

You have a reason for being excited about this change; others must know what it is. One division director told her staff, "We are facing major challenges over the next few years; I don't believe we are structured to address them adequately. I want us to work together to develop a division that can continually adapt and respond to new challenges." She backed up her statement about a need for change with tangible information about the business climate. She called in senior management to present its views of the future.

A clear statement provides focus and energizes people. Some get excited by the possibility implied in the statement. For others, it raises fear and doubt, and their energy is mobilized as resistance. In both cases you bring them into sync with you on your Cycle of Change.

When senior management at Deloitte & Touche decided to seek ways to retain and advance more women, reaction within the firm was strong. As you might imagine, some said, "It's about time." Others were skeptical of the leaders' sincerity. Still others believed it would not serve the best interests of clients.

Your statement needs to be clear and impassioned. Clarity lets people know what you are thinking; passion tells them why this is important to you. The stronger the statement, the stronger the reaction. (Beware of tepid statements like, "My goal is for our company to be the industry leader by embracing quality and customer service." That's not enough for even the strongest potential supporters to get on board. Nor will it give people who might react deeply against it enough information to react—yet.)

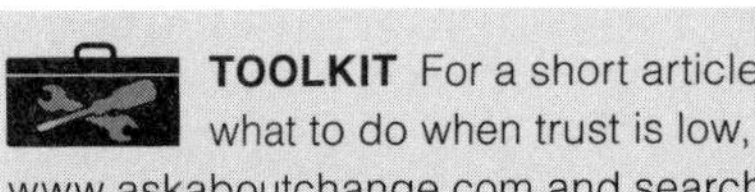

TOOLKIT For a short article on what to do when trust is low, visit www.askaboutchange.com and search for **when trust is low**.

Step 2: Analyze What You Just Learned

Make a list. And put each thing you learned into one or more of the six boxes.

Analyze what you've got.

1. Convene a meeting with a few people you trust and who will speak candidly. Prior to the meeting give people the raw data from surveys, informal conversations, and other sources. It often helps to separate information by groups: information from field offices, information from first-line supervisors, etc.
2. Teach people the three levels of support and resistance. You can do that in five to ten minutes.
3. Post a large copy of The List on a flip chart or white board. You may want to post more than one list so that you can separate what you learned by group (for example, one list for field offices, another for first-line supervisors, and so forth).
4. Invite the group to help you put the raw data into categories. Remember that some items might belong in more than one category. When in doubt, make a guess and put a question mark beside that item.
5. Take a few minutes to allow everyone to quietly read over The List.

The List

(Level 1) Ways in Which They Understand	Ways in Which They Don't Get It
(Level 2) Reactions in Favor of the Idea	Reactions Against the Idea
(Level 3) Indications That They Trust Me (Us)	Indications That They Don't Trust Me (Us)

Discuss:

- What's your first reaction to this information?
- What stands out to you?
- Where is there hope?
- Where are the challenges?
- What should we do? (This leads to the next step—act.)

Step 3: Act on What You Just Learned

Peggy was head of nursing at a major hospital. The executive team, of which she was a part, decided to hire nonlicensed employees to perform simple routine nursing tasks like drawing blood and changing simple wound dressings. She believed that some nurses would be upset by that decision and she wanted to have a conversation with them. She decided to meet with the nurses in smaller groups. She told me that if she got up in front of all 350-some nurses, it could easily turn into a presentation.

We came up with a simple design for a meeting. Each meeting was scheduled to last ninety minutes. Approximately thirty nurses would be invited to each meeting until all the nurses had an opportunity to attend.

She began each meeting by describing the rationale for the decision and what the decision would look like in practice. She talked about how many non-licensed employees would be hired, the departments where they would be placed, the timeline for this, etc.

I asked people to talk with one or two other people and identify questions of clarification. They talked in small groups for a few minutes and then Peggy addressed those questions.

Now that the nurses understood what was going to happen (Level 1), I asked the nurses to discuss their reactions in those same small groups. Most groups said that they were worried about job security. Peggy had anticipated that and told them that concerned her too, but that she believed this decision would actually strengthen job security and explained why. She added that she did not have a crystal ball and couldn't predict the future.

They expressed concern over losing their own licenses. If one of these new employees messed up, the nurse on duty could lose his or her license. Another group said they were worried about quality of care for their patients.

In each instance, Peggy took what they said seriously. It was clear to me that she respected the nurses and what they had to say. She had earned their trust well before this meeting. One example: If she had an announcement to make, she met with nurses during the day shift and scheduled another meeting with the night shift during their time at work. Not asking nurses to come in when they should be sleeping builds a lot of trust.

As people talked about their Level 2 concerns, she asked them a simple question: Would some of you be willing to work with me to ensure that the new hires are brought on board in a way that keeps quality of care high? That our licenses are never in jeopardy? That actually strengthens job security?

Peggy made no promises, but engaged her staff around the issues that were important to all of them. In that meeting she addressed all three steps—assess, analyze, and act.

Workout as a Way to Act

After the massive downsizing in the 1980s that earned him the unflattering nickname "Neutron Jack," former GE chairman Jack Welch asked those attending the company's Management Institute what the reaction to these changes was out in the field. Managers told him of their deep concerns: people were overwhelmed trying to do the work of those who had gone, and stress was high.

On the helicopter back to corporate headquarters, Welch turned to the institute's director and told him to come up with some way to work out these issues. By inviting people to speak the truth, he heard things that prompted the development of GE's Workout Program. (See the sidebar earlier in this chapter for a description of the process.)

Workout is a gathering in which the company's employees—sometimes all of them—tell management what they think. It's not easy or fun, but it can put a lot of information on the table quickly. A middle manager described how it worked in one plant.

> We were getting screws from one supplier that were not so good. The bits would break off the screw heads, and scratch the product, and cut people's hands—we had one guy get eighteen stitches. Tempers flared, but management never went and fixed it. They said, "Okay, we'll go get you some screws from the good supplier." But then the bad screws would always reappear. So a shop steward named Jimmy stood up at Workout and told the story. This guy was a maverick, a rock thrower, a naysayer. He wanted to test us, to see whether we really wanted to change.

> He knew what he was talking about. And he explained the solution, which had to do with how deep the bit could be inserted into the screw head. We listened, then asked, "Okay, what do you suggest?"
>
> He replied, "We need to go tell the supplier what the problems are."
>
> Well, I was nervous about it, but I decided to charter a plane to fly Jimmy and a couple other guys to the plant in Virginia where they made the bad screws.
>
> Jimmy got the problem fixed, and it sent a powerful message to everyone here. He became a leader instead of a maverick simply because we gave them the forum and allowed him to have some ownership.[2]

A Workout-style meeting can be quite effective if management truly wants to hear the truth. But it takes tremendous fortitude to stand in front of a large room inviting criticism.

A warning: Workout can be misused. If Workout becomes a ticket that you need to have punched to prove you are a good leader, people will pick up on that insincerity. If the leader holds a Workout and everything seems to go well, but afterwards nothing changes, Workout will turn into a joke. Only use Workout if you are prepared to listen deeply to what people say and then act on it.

BRIDGING THE GAP

Slap-Your-Head Obvious Solution

If the potential problem was obvious, you probably wouldn't have gotten into this mess. You would have picked up the warning signals long ago.

Lack of Knowledge and Lack of Skill

Business schools don't usually teach us to work with resistance. Intense Level 2 fears and Level 3 distrust can be frightening since you are the target for the anger, rage, and confusion that gets released.

I urge you to reread chapter 3, "Why People Support You and Why They Resist." And then read it again as you reflect on a meeting that went bad, or an encounter in the hall that made matters worse. The better you understand the reasons why people support or resist you, the more options you'll have. And then practice trying to bring out the positive side of Levels 1, 2, and 3 in relatively safe situations. There is no shortage of opportunities to practice at work, while shopping, traveling, and maybe (but very carefully) at home.

Get interested in what's not being said as it relates to the change you are leading. Look around you for clues that let you know if things are on track or off track. Notice the subtle and not-so-subtle signals. When you are ready to find out what's going on at the three levels, go slowly. Be kind to yourself. Don't get up in front of 100 people and ask, "So, what's on your mind?" You might hear more than your fragile ego can handle and out will come some Wes Craven–style knee-jerk reaction.

A good coach can be very helpful in increasing the knowledge and skills required to get things back on track. And a coach who knows you well can be especially helpful in keeping you out of potential knee-jerk situations.

Competing Beliefs

Some beliefs that work against your goal of getting the change back on track could be "Something really bad will happen if I even mention the issues out loud," or "Anything I do will only make matters worse," or "I'll look like a fool." These beliefs can easily lead to hidden vows like "I am committed to keeping things under control at all costs." Or, "I am committed to muscling through the resistance and making this change move ahead no matter what." You can see how "muscling through" works against a desire to build support for change with your staff. Chapter 11, "Moving Toward Mastery," can help you develop a plan to handle the competing desire to get things back on track and a deep concern that you'll make matters worse if you try.

Context

If you work in a Theory X organization (see chapter 5) where people are treated like objects and means to an end, then you'll probably find little or no support for digging deep and finding out what the very real human concerns are. You may even get punished for daring to go where no manager has gone before. When others look at your actions through a Theory X lens, they may see you as weak. This creates a powerful dilemma for you. If you do openly explore the reasons things are off track, you may put your own reputation at risk. If you don't find out why things are off track, your chances of seeing this project succeed have diminished greatly.

When you look at the context you work in, the need for knowledge and skill takes on a new significance. You've got to know how to work effectively in your unique organization. Textbooks and theories will only take you so far. Consider finding men and women in your organization who are leading in ways that you admire and ask for their advice. Buy them lots of lunches. Keep them happy. More than likely, you will need to call on them again and again. The wisdom they possess could be invaluable to you.

HOW YOU CAN TELL YOU ARE BACK ON TRACK

When your car goes into a ditch during a snowstorm, it is going to be pretty obvious when you have pulled it out and you are back on the road headed toward your destination. Same goes for getting back on track when major change starts to derail. Ask yourself, are you on the road again?

Signs you are back on track:

- You will be paying closer attention to things like the tasks involved in Keeping Change Alive.
- You won't be experiencing what a friend aptly described as ". . . taking an acid bath." Your stomach will know if you are still embroiled in the chaos of resistance.
- You and all the teams working on this project will be meeting deadlines.
- Complaints and questions will be focused on concern over how everyone can reach objectives and goals in the most efficient and effective way possible.

Natural Change

An Interview with Margaret Wheatley

Margaret Wheatley is the author of Turning to One Another *and the best-selling* Leadership and the New Science, *an exploration of the ways in which the discoveries in sub-atomic physics and chaos theory might be applied in organizations. Since resistance is a part of the natural world, it seems that her thinking might help illuminate the conversation on the subject.*

RM: You've written that the Newtonian mechanistic model hinders our ability to change.

MW: It is an absolute mental block created by our machine images. Machines only change within very narrow limits. I think that we don't understand at all how well equipped we are as living organisms to deal with change in a creative way, so that resistance becomes a much different issue—minimized in some ways. I absolutely believe that the whole focus on resistance to change is just a by-product of very bad change processes. The resistance we are experiencing in organizations says nothing about human nature or our innate ability to deal with change in a changing world.

RM: What is resistance in your view?

MW: Resistance is people's assertion of their identity as they presently construct it.

RM: So if current change processes threaten that identity, how should we view change?

MW: The world is self-organizing. Everywhere we look, we see change going on—change, growth and development, and increasing complexity. All of these things are evident everywhere and they are evident in our own lives. Then we get into organizations in which change becomes not an ability, but just a huge problem for us. I think we need to stop looking at human nature negatively and look at our change processes with much more discernment. We do have a self-organizing capacity in us, which means that we will change in order to maintain ourselves. Change is not foreign. In the natural world change is not a singular event you try to live through, it's just the way things are. I think the saying "People don't resist change, they resist being changed" sums it up.

RM: What are the implications if people don't resist change itself, but only resist being changed?

MW: A person in one organization said resistance to change is like a mantra we feed ourselves: "In every team meeting we get together and spend the first twenty minutes saying change is hard. People resist change." This is an unexamined belief about human nature. Our assumptions about stability and the promises of equilibrium were all false promises and that is not how life is. If people participate from the beginning of the change they are able to re-identify or change their identity so that it doesn't feel threatening.

PART III

Narrowing the Gap the Next Time

"Don't spend time beating on a wall, hoping to transform it into a door."

—COCO CHANEL
Fashion Designer

My hope is that the first nine chapters of this book gave you ways to think about planning and implementing change so that you can lead change with a much greater chance of succeeding.

This final section shows you how to expand the application of your knowledge to other components of change, like hiring and monitoring the work of consultants and selecting people to lead change within your organization. It ends with an exploration of what it takes to move toward mastery as a leader of change.

10

Expanding Your Ability to Apply What You've Learned

When you're finished changing, you're finished.

—Benjamin Franklin

Lance has carried a copy of the cycle around in his wallet for years. He told me that he uses it as a reminder to pay attention to where everyone around the table—including himself—is on the Cycle of Change. That instant assessment often gives him information about what he needs to do next.

Since you made it this far in the book, I will assume that you are finding ways to apply what you are learning to some project that is in the works today. I thought it might be helpful to end the book by showing you a range of ways you can apply the Cycle of Change and the three levels of support and resistance.

You might think of this chapter as the recipe portion of the book. I don't expect you to be interested in all these recipes today, but you may find one or two that you want to try out.

Here are some of the ways of expanding the reach of what you've just learned:

- Working with your own team
- Evaluating an approach to change that you are thinking about using
- Working with consultants
- Choosing someone to lead a project
- Supervising someone who is leading a change
- Guiding your own actions

WORKING WITH YOUR OWN TEAM

A regional office of an insurance company hung the Cycle of Change in their main conference room. I asked why. They told me that it helped them stay aligned with people within their own region and with headquarters and other regions across the country.

TOOLKIT For a podcast on how to teach this approach to leading change to your own team, visit www.askaboutchange.com and search for **teach this approach**.

A department head in a government agency taught the cycle and the three levels to his staff. As they embarked on a major change, he told his staff, "I'm going to be In the Dark for a couple of weeks trying to figure out where things stand. As a result, you're going to be In the Dark as well." This heads-up helped keep apprehension at bay.

Teach the Cycle and the Three Levels

I recommend teaching people these two models. In my experience, people grasp the cycle and the three levels very quickly. If you devoted just forty-five minutes of a staff meeting to teach the cycle and the levels, you should be able to give people enough to get started.

It's important for you and your team to begin to apply what you learn immediately. Don't wait for the next meeting, do it today. (It is surprising how quickly knowledge fades when it isn't reinforced.) You might say, "So let's use the cycle to look at the new software project. Where do we seem to be on the cycle? Where would we put our customers? Our internal suppliers? Headquarters?" And then turn your attention to the Level 1, 2, and 3 issues that are working for you and those that could hinder movement forward.

Take a look at the Resources page at the end of this book. On my website (www.askaboutchange.com) you will find a lot of free resources that can help you teach this approach to others.

Don't worry about teaching it perfectly. Better to get it out there so people can begin to use it. You can work on the fine points as others read portions of this book or take advantage of the free resources.

Use These Lenses as You Plan and Implement Changes

You may find that the four stages in the cycle—Making a Compelling Case for Change, Getting Started on the Right Foot, Keeping Change Alive, and Getting Back on Track—provide all the structure you need to plan and implement a change. If so, force yourselves to stick with this model. For example, if the work is at the Making a Compelling Case for Change stage, then keep your focus there until it's done. In other words, stay at that stage until you know you've made a case.

Reread the chapter that covers the stage where you are working. And bring in other resources that you know apply at that stage.

The temptation will be to move too quickly. You'll make a half-hearted attempt to make a case. You'll think that your epic PowerPoint show replete with bullet points and clip art did the job, and you won't take time to see if you truly finished the work of that stage.

EVALUATING AN APPROACH TO CHANGE

You may already have a change process that you love to use. Great. Don't switch horses now, but make sure that the process you follow covers all the things you need to do to build support for your new initiative.

Or perhaps you are about to start a very technical change, like creating a software system that touches all parts of your organization. You need a game plan that reflects the very specific challenges associated with this new enterprise-wide software. I encourage you to use the approaches you've just learned—the Cycle of Change and the three levels of support and resistance—as a lens to look at the human side of change at every stage.

Here are some things to consider:

Making a Compelling Case for Change

You may need to back up and add this stage into your plan if you skipped it. If so, read chapter 6 again, "How to Make a Compelling Case for Change."

As you make a case, make sure you let people know if you have already created a vision or goals and a plan for moving to Results on the cycle. You want them to know what led you to make that decision. Keep your eyes open so you'll know when you've actually made a compelling case.

Getting Started

Most approaches to change cover the things that need to be addressed at this stage. What may be missing though is a strategy for engaging others in a meaningful way. Lip service involvement won't do.

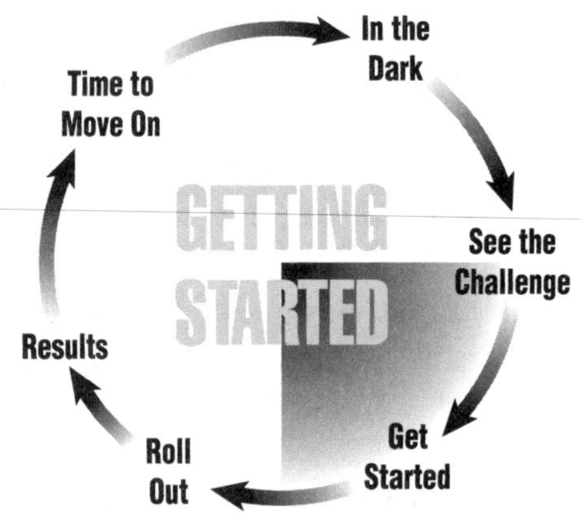

Make sure people understand the plan and then ask for their help in adapting it to your unique organizational circumstances.

1. What do we need to do to make sure this plan gets us where we want to go?
2. What are the pitfalls we might encounter?
3. How will we deal with these potential problems if they occur?
4. How can we avoid the pitfalls in the first place?

Invite people to help influence the change that will affect them. You are asking people to roll up their sleeves and become part of the planning. That's a big deal.

Keeping the Change Alive

Make sure that the plan covers the items covered in chapter 8, "How to Keep Change Alive." Technical and financial plans look rational because they are filled with lots of numbers and details. You could be lulled into thinking that everything is taken care of. As important as those technical elements of the plan might be in implementing something like Six Sigma, to take just one example, you've got to have a plan that includes things like senior leadership's commitment. Without paying attention to the softer items that keep change alive, the change will fade away well before you ever get to Results. Ask anyone if they remember TQM (Total Quality Management). It was a great idea that only got fully implemented in a few organizations. In others, quality improvement became another failed change on a heap of past failed initiatives.

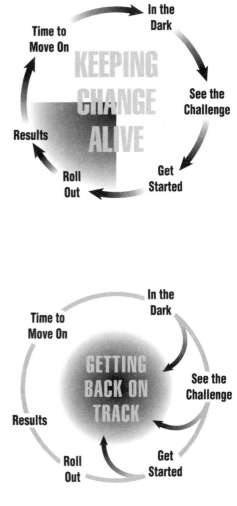

Getting Back on Track

Going into a change with a prepackaged plan may create an illusion that nothing can go wrong. But you know as well as I, life doesn't work that neatly. The same Level 1, Level 2, and Level 3 issues that impact other types of change can affect this one as well. The problem is that you could easily get seduced by the glossy manual you are following. It may lead you to believe that the change will be neat and linear. You say to yourself, "If we are on activity 128 today, then surely 129 will occur tomorrow like clockwork."

WORKING WITH CONSULTANTS

Everything covered in the last section, "Evaluating an Approach to Change," applies when you are working with consultants.

In addition . . .

Beware of consultants bearing PowerPoint. It is easy to become intimidated by high-powered consulting firms. Because they speak so articulately, dress so nicely, and have such swell binders, they can create a false sense of comfort that things will go smoothly.

Consultants can bring a lot of value to your project. Many are experts in your particular type of organization. Others have expertise in particular types of changes. Still others specialize in getting people involved in the process. These are all potentially valuable resources.

The problem comes when you hand over your managerial responsibilities to these outsiders. You are hired to make the decisions. (At least I hope you are.) Good consultants won't try to usurp that, but they will fill a leadership vacuum in a heartbeat.

It's your job to lead the change. So consider this short list:

- Use the Cycle of Change to make sure that the ideas and plans consultants suggest make sense with regard to where you and others are on the cycle.
- Be willing to be influenced by their advice. That's why you hired them.
- Only work with consultants who are willing to be influenced by you as well. If they roll their eyes when you speak, change the game or change consultants.

Keeping the Change Alive

Pay particular attention to Roll Out on the cycle. This is the point where the change goes live. All the plans are in place. People have had the training they need. You turn the switch and the lights go on.

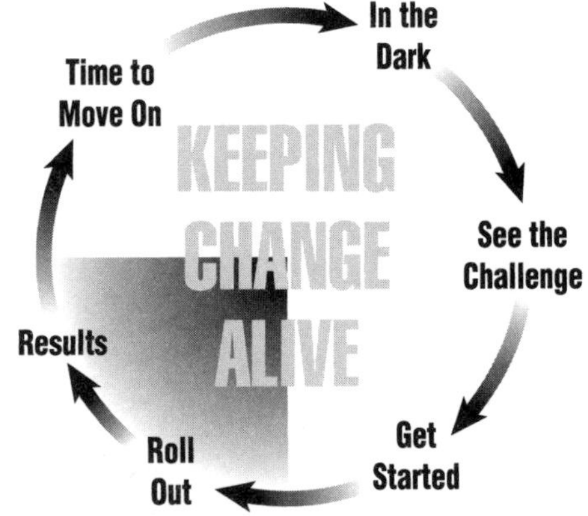

This is the point where many consulting contracts end. The consultants did what you asked. They got you to the point where plans turn into implementation.

But the problem is that you haven't gotten any benefit out of this project yet. You need to get to Results so that the change is no longer a change, but a part of how you now do business—and you are beginning to see tangible outcomes from all that effort.

Write a contract with consultants that includes their involvement to help get you to Results. Or, make sure that their plans actively engage people so that when they leave town, your own team has the commitment, capacity, and resources to ensure the change stays alive and vital. (I am sometimes amazed at how freely companies spend lots of money on consultants to help plan and implement change, but provide next to nothing to the internal groups and individuals who are supposed to lead the change.)

CHOOSING SOMEONE TO LEAD A PROJECT

Past performance is the best predictor of what people will do in the future. Say Maria is an individual contributor and she does outstanding work. Since she knows so much about the technical part of her work, she may seem like the ideal person to lead a project team. Maybe, maybe not. Ask yourself, what evidence do I have that this person can

- build support and commit to working on something new?
- be curious about what others think and allow him/herself to be influenced by others?
- manage the human, financial, and technical elements of a complex change?
- deal with resistance in a way that turns opposition into support?
- think on his/her feet and shift course quickly? (Not in a knee-jerk fashion but thoughtfully, like a martial artist.)

Leading change is challenging. If it weren't, the success rate would be much higher. Reading books is fine. Going to training can be OK too, but only if this person seems to have an aptitude that suggests that she might be a good fit for this challenging role. Otherwise, you are taking too big a risk.

SUPERVISING SOMEONE WHO IS LEADING A CHANGE

The people leading changes in your organization need to know that you've got their backs. Here are some of the big things you can do:

- **Delegate clearly and responsibly.** As one manager told me, "Cut out the word 'just,'" as in "If you could just take this on along with the other things you are doing." If you want a new task done well then make sure the people who are leading have the time and resources to do it right. When you pile on a new responsibility, something's got to give. And with people who really care about their work, what they may give up is the rest of their lives.

- **Be a vocal advocate.** If the leader of change wants you to reinforce the message so that everyone knows that you are still committed to this project, say yes to what he asks.

I was in a meeting in a company that had instituted a diversity program so that when it came time to promote people into executive ranks there weren't just a bunch of white guys in the queue. Some of the managers and executives didn't see how this helped the business. Besides, it took them off focus with regard to the mission of their business. The facilitator was having a hard time of it until one vice-president turned to his colleagues and said, "I was in a meeting with the chairman last week and he's 100 percent behind this." Because people knew that the chairman wasn't a flavor-of-the-month kind of guy and only got behind projects that he believed were good for the company, the tone of that meeting shifted dramatically. People leaned in and started to work on how to make this new initiative work in their region.

Making sure that everyone knows you are doing what it takes to make sure this change is a success is critically important.

- **Run interference.** Others may try to pull your change leader off into other directions. Don't let it happen. Be the one to say no. And be the one to make sure that he has the resources needed from beginning to end.
- **Be available.** Let this leader know that your door truly is always open. Prove it by checking in just to see if he needs something.
- **Pay attention to what you reward and what you ignore.** If the company still rewards the old ways of behaving, you will sabotage the efforts of this leader. Also, if you ignore this project, you will send a message that it has slipped off your radar and is no longer a top priority.

GUIDING YOUR OWN ACTIONS

The more you use the ideas in this book, the more comfortable you'll get applying them. Here are a few things that can help:

- Make sure you understand the cycle. An easy way to begin to see the cycle in action is to watch someone else's change unfold. You'll learn a lot about where people are on the cycle and ways to work with those differences effectively and ineffectively. And face it, it's fun to watch others mess up.
- Use the three levels of support and resistance as you watch conversations unfold. It's hard to learn to work with resistance in the moment. Just look around. In virtually every meeting you attend you will see the three levels writ large.
- Stay open and curious. As my old friend Edwin Nevis says when faced with a surprising response from someone, "Isn't it interesting?" This simple question to yourself can allow you to stay open to the possibility that this person isn't a raving idiot and might have something valuable to say.
- My buddy Herb Stevenson often advises his clients to "pause, reflect, and act." This tiny pause can stop you from giving into knee-jerk reactions, and that sometimes can make all the difference.

You know what they say about the best laid plans? Well, get used to it. The stages in the life of a change will likely occur in order. And with good planning, things may never get off track. But you never know. Context matters. You may miss seeing something important, like the woman with the umbrella. Or that butterfly flaps or belches, and you've got to adjust.

The men and women who lead change well understand that the process is more like jazz than classical music. There is an agreed-upon structure, but how things play out can depend as much on your ability to improvise as anything else.

11

Moving Toward Mastery

"I've learned from my mistakes. I'm sure that I could repeat them exactly."

—Peter Cook, from "The Frog and Peach" routine

When National Endowment for the Arts Grand Master and world-renowned jazz saxophonist James Moody was on tour a couple of years ago, every day he would get on the band's bus and study music as they rode to the next gig. He was eighty-two at the time. One of the younger musicians was taken by this and said, "This must be fun for you, James." Moody looked at him and said, "What's fun got to do with it? It's what you've got to do."

James Moody got it right. The people who learn to do anything well never achieve mastery in their own minds. They keep working on it. The leaders I know who lead and manage change well would nod in agreement with Moody's comments.

As I started to work on this new edition of the book, I interviewed a number of people who worked inside organizations. I asked them to tell about a time when they led a change successfully—but getting the support they needed was not a foregone conclusion. The changes they led ranged from large organizational changes that demanded the support of the most senior leaders and external customers, to creating a guiding coalition[1] for their organization, to getting a buy-in to new software, and much more.

In spite of the differences in the types of changes, the underlying stories were pretty similar. Here's what stood out to me:

- They all knew their stuff. They knew what they needed to know about the type of change they were leading. For example, if it was a new software application, they knew what it would take to get something like that up and running.
- They had a theory of change in mind. It may have been a theory they learned in a book; at other times it was their own theory. But in each case, it seemed that they understood the theory they used well. It helped guide their actions. They may not have actually called it a theory, but as they spoke, it was clear they had principles and beliefs that guided their actions.
- They understood how to work in their unique cultures. Often they knew the players they needed to influence. In other cases, they were quick studies when they first met those people and adapted their approach to new and often unique circumstances.
- They had good instincts. In tough situations, they chose well. These good instincts were born of knowledge, observation, and practice. Their theories provided a backdrop that supported making good choices.
- Their mindsets worked for them. One told me, "I have always wanted to have a positive impact in the world." Another told me that Getting the Right People on the Bus (a principle in Collins' *Good to Great*) guided his actions. What came across is that they trusted themselves and they trusted the capability and goodness of the people they worked with.
- They all had tenacity. Things didn't go smoothly all the time for all of them, but they stuck with it.
- Some even seemed to have a good time with all the challenges. One leader delighted in telling me how the person he needed to influence told him that he didn't like him or who he represented. You could tell that this leader enjoyed the challenge of turning intense Level 3 hostility into support. (And he did earn the stakeholder's support, by the way.)

My goal in this chapter is to help you move toward mastery of bridging the gap between knowledge and action. I'll cover intention, what gets in the way of acting on that intention, how to work through those barriers, and how to develop disciplined practice so that you can continually increase your use of skills and your effectiveness.

SHIFT YOUR INTENTION, CHANGE THE OUTCOME

Sounds a little woo-woo, right? Bear with me. I think you'll see just how valuable this notion of shifting intentions can be.

There is a tendency to focus on tools and techniques as we try to get better in any endeavor, whether it's music, sports, graphic arts, or leadership. But skills alone don't create mastery. I've worked with musicians who can play fast and high and yet it's hard to find the music within that flurry of sound. Clearly, we need to have skills, but that's not where it should start. It starts with clear intention.

1. Clarify Your Intention

If I could follow you around and ask you what your intention is at various moments as you lead a major change, you might be surprised at your responses. Getting past the fact that most of us don't think a lot about our intention before we act, you might say, "Well, my goal was to . . ."

Goals and intentions are different. A goal is what we want to accomplish. Intention is the way in which we want to meet that goal. So, for example, let's say my goal is to get a project completed on time and within budget. Then you ask, "So, Rick, what's your intention?" And I draw a blank. That lack of knowing my intention could mark the difference between success and failure.

If my goal is to bring this project in on time and within budget, there are many ways in which I could *intend* to get that accomplished. For example, my intention might be . . .

- to get everyone engaged in planning and implementation, or
- to seek advice from people I respect, or
- to demand compliance from everyone, or
- to hire mercenaries (or consultants) to make sure the job gets done right.

Each of those intentions brings with it very different sets of behaviors from me and from those who fall under the spell of this way of working.

Ask yourself, "What would I like my intention to be when I lead a major change?" Here are some things to prompt your thinking:

- to learn from successes and failures
- to be willing to be influenced by others
- to believe in people's capacity to change

2. Find Your Pattern

Most of us have habitual ways of doing things. Our intentions usually don't change dramatically unless we choose to revise them.

Write with some detail a story of how you led a change. Don't evaluate as you tell your story, just tell it. For example, don't write, "We held a planning meeting, a bunch of people came, it worked pretty well, and then we assigned tasks. . . ." Rather, "I worked with my senior team to design the agenda for a planning meeting that involved close to 100 people from various functions and levels in the organization. Not everyone on my team agreed with my desire to get so many people involved. We discussed the pros and cons of various approaches. . . ." The difference is that the second example provides more context. As you recall that story, you should feel like you are reliving the experience.

Now step back and imagine that this is someone else's story. What would you say his or her overall intentions were along the way? In particular, look at:

- how you got things started
- who you included and who you either chose to exclude or "forgot" to include
- how you responded when people pushed back with some emotion
- points where your leadership was put to a test

What did you do during those times?

This retrospective look at how you lead change can give you a much better picture of your intentions. Arthur Schopenhauer (1788–1860) wrote, "It is in the trifles—when he is off guard—that a man best reveals his character." (Same goes for women, but apparently Schopenhauer didn't know that.)

3. Do a Reality Check

Invite someone you trust to listen to your story. Then ask this trusted friend what he or she thinks your intentions seem to be at every step you describe.

Why is this necessary? There is one very good reason: we're often deluded. Most of us rate our driving skills, our ability to communicate, and many other things well above average. (And I can tell you that, except for me, almost all the drivers I see on the road are below average.) So saying what we think we do doesn't always equate with what we actually do.

A friend who is willing to speak candidly can help you see any gap between your description of your intentions and what others see.

4. Get Under the Hood

Sometimes you've got to lift up the hood to see why the car isn't running the way you'd like. In *Immunity to Change*, Robert Kegan and Lisa Lahey[2] invite people to identify what they truly want and then list all the things that they are doing or not doing that work against that goal.

That's a great thing to do with regard to your intentions as a leader of change. Identify the things you currently are doing—or not doing—that get in the way of embracing that way of approaching change.

Getting under the hood keeps you and me from pretending that we are living consistently with what we espouse.

Kegan and Lahey consistently find five benefits to get at these assumption or beliefs behind their actions:

1. People succeed in changing their mindsets, which Kagen and Lahey describe as "meaning making system[s] that shape thoughts and feelings."
2. They become "keen and focused observers of their own thoughts, emotions, and behaviors."
3. "Changes to their mindsets are always in the direction of seeing and feeling more possibilities."
4. "They take focused risks and build a new set of muscles" which are based on real data about their performance rather than on some fantasy or old picture of who they were and what they were capable of.
5. "They experience mastery, more options, wider control, and greater degrees of freedom."[3]

In their book, they describe a process for examining these "hidden commitments." They believe that these commitments have as much power as our conscious and "more noble" intentions. For example, say that I want to be influenced by your thinking on a particular issue that is near and dear to both of us. Once I scratch the surface, I realize that I am also committed to preserving my status as the brightest guy in the room. (This is a rather common set of conflicting intentions that you find in many organizations.)

When I understand how different intentions are competing inside of me, then I've got options.

I urge you to read my interview with Bob Kegan and Lisa Laskow Lahey in this chapter. (And I highly recommend their book. They guide you through every step in the process of examining your goals, identifying competing hidden commitments, and the assumptions that lie beneath it all. Then they explain ways to begin to change how you look at things and how you respond.)

5. Find Your Support

If you want to shift your intentions to reinforce your goals, you'll probably need support. And for Americans like me—who grew up on cowboy movies with the lone gunman cleaning up the wicked town—get over it. These can be entertaining myths, but that's all they are. Most of us need support.

I encourage you to find someone (a buddy, a coach, a partner) to help you talk about and think through the following:

- Do you have the skills you need to act on this new set of intentions? If not, what can you do to identify and then develop those skills? All of the things covered in this book should be a pretty good basis for establishing a skills baseline. You might glance at chapter 2 for a few minutes and ask yourself if you've really got the Cycle of Change (or some other way of organizing your thinking about change) under your belt. Then move on to chapters 3 through 9 asking the same questions. You probably noticed that all of those chapters end with a Bridging the Gap section that usually begins with just asking you to pay attention. Jumping to action before you know the territory and what challenges it might possess can be risky.
- What do you need from the environment where you work in order to realize these intentions? Kurt Lewin, a pioneer in group and organizational psychology, said that behavior is a func-

tion of the person *and* his or her environment. Think about Ted Conover at Sing Sing. It was Conover, the person, plus the environment that determined how he behaved at work and then at home. When Philip Zimbardo said that the barrel was bad at Abu Ghraib and not just a few bad apples, he captured Lewin's thinking perfectly.

- If you live in a culture like the U.S. that is very individualistic, then expanding your view to include context or environment might be a challenge. Reviewing chapter 5, "Ignore the Context at Your Peril," might be a good place to start.

6. Determine How You Will Reinforce This New Way of Thinking

If all this talk about intentions is new to you, then it's probably going to be new for the people you work with. Inadvertently, people and organizations try to keep the old status quo intact. This is another place where you will need to find support from others.

You may need to find a way to keep reminding yourself of your new intentions. For instance, you "believe in the capacity of people (including you) to rise to challenges." You are in a meeting and someone blows up. They point directly at your face and say, "This is the dumbest idea you've ever come up with. And you're an idiot too." You feel blood surging through your body. So before you allow your knee-jerk to materialize as the Incredible Hulk, how will you remember your newly minted intention of being open to different points of view? Tough, isn't it? It's worth thinking about before you are put to the test.

Years ago, when I first began working as a consultant, I agreed to facilitate a retreat in which management and staff within a state education agency would explore issues impeding their working together. The opening hours of the meeting seemed to go pretty well, but then the wind shifted. Without warning, people started criticizing me—and I was just the facilitator. What was going on?

TOOLKIT For a podcast that reviews this approach to leading change, visit www.askaboutchange.com and search for **Intro to Change Without Migraines**.

To deal with their resistance, I drew on the conventional approaches. I reminded them of my role: "I'm not here to take sides. I'm a trained professional." (That's a knee-jerk reaction.) They would have none of it. The attacks continued. I tried another tactic—shifting to the next topic on the agenda. (Yet another knee-jerk.) That didn't work either. They weren't moving. And on it went until, mercifully, the time came for a break.

Fortunately, I had had the good sense to invite Lloyd Richards, one of the most experienced consultants I knew, to join me. During the break, I pulled Lloyd aside and asked, "What am I doing wrong?" He smiled and said, "Rick, there is a thunderstorm out there. You didn't create the storm, but since you are the highest point, you are drawing all its electricity. You've got a choice. Either you can continue to stand there like an old tree and take all the hits, or you can be like a lightning rod and allow the electricity to pass through you."

His advice worked. After the break, I used that metaphor to guide my actions and purposely drew even more hits. I copied their questions, concerns, and criticisms on the board. Once the storm had passed and the air had cleared, they were able to examine the issues under calmer skies.

That image has stuck with me for some thirty years. When I can recall it quickly enough, it helps me stick with what I intended and not get trapped by the things that trigger my knee-jerks.

You must invite the storm. Simply listening to the distant thunder won't do. You must be willing to stand atop a hill and bring the storm to you.

Our Immunity to Change

An Interview with Robert Kegan and Lisa Laskow Lahey

Robert Kegan and Lisa Laskow Lahey are coauthors of How the Way We Talk Can Change the Way We Work, *as well as* Immunity to Change. *Bob is a professor in Adult Learning and Professional Development in Harvard University's Graduate School of Education. Lisa is the associate director of Harvard's Change Leadership Group. And they are the founders of Minds at Work (www.mindsatwork.com).*

RM: What is "immunity to change"?

RK: What if the mind, like the body, has an immune system that works ceaselessly to keep us out of trouble; that regularly protects us from disaster—but, on occasion, also puts us at great risk by fighting against new material trying to get in because it mistakenly perceives a threat or danger?

LLL: The idea immediately recasts the familiar situation of our inability to make changes we sincerely want to make. For example, we worked with an administrator who knows he is too critical and aggressive in team arguments. He sincerely wants to tone it down but fails repeatedly. "I just get so annoyed that I can't help myself." He thinks he doesn't change because of his limitations or weakness. We think we can't stop overeating because we lack willpower. We think can't change the way we do our jobs because we are set in our ways.

RM: And what does your approach suggest?

RK: When the administrator went through our "X-ray activity," which helped him see what is normally invisible, he had a whole different picture. He happened to be a person of color working in a predominantly white team. He came to see that whenever he felt too much a part of the team it made him uncomfortable, like he was selling out. He would get critical and overly assertive because it successfully moved him back to the margins of his team where he was far more comfortable!

LLL: He wasn't "failing to change" because of some weakness. He was, without realizing it, very successfully fulfilling what we call a "hidden commitment"—to not feel co-opted, to stay on the margins.

RM: And the hidden commitment is self-protective?

RK: Always. That is the work of an immune system: it takes care of you; it's on the job all the time; and you are completely unaware of it.

RM: So how can we overcome our immunity to change? We don't want to give up our immune systems.

LLL: We *shouldn't* give them up. An immune system is a beautiful, intelligent thing. But we can *alter* our immune systems. They can take a different form. They can be less distorting, have fewer "false alarms." We overcome our current immune systems, first, by learning about them and the assumptions that undergird them. For example, the aggressive administrator has the assumption that he cannot be well-integrated into his team and still feel strongly aligned with his people.

RK: And the second step is to *test* these assumptions. For example, what first experiment might the administrator run to see if his assumption is really valid? One test leads to another, and before long, the immune system has begun to change. He is still taking good care of himself, but he can alter those overly aggressive behaviors.

RM: Most people don't like to look at what they think of as their own deficiencies or weaknesses. And they—me included—start to put up defenses. Yet, as I watched both of you work, I was struck by how easy it was for people to engage with this process and look at their so-called deficiencies with laughter and the joy of recognition. And I think your respect for people allowed this to occur. Do you agree with that?

LLL: I've found that our approach allows people to be much more generous towards themselves. Seeing that you are engaged in these "brilliant" behaviors can allow you to shift away from the self-recriminations and beating up on yourself. To me, it's a gift to help people see that the problem they're trying to solve is much different than the one they think they're trying to solve. When you can help them reframe it like that, it does shift from being mad at yourself to, "Oh! That's really interesting! I'm being very good to myself."

BK: I think that the respect you're talking about is more the *result* of something rather than an initial starting point. I don't begin by telling myself, "I should be respectful." If you take seriously the fact that when people continue to do things that run counter to even some of their most urgent and dearly desired goals, that we are implicating their anxiety management system—which is really what an immune system for the mind is. If you start out with that notion, then what you're really looking at is people's *courage*. The respect that you're experiencing might be just the natural consequence of being moved by learning of the secret dangers which we are all so bravely facing and dealing with every second of every day.

RM: I really don't want this interview to seem like an infomercial, but I believe the focus of this work is so important to people leading change that I hope readers will read your book *Immunity to Change* carefully and complete the process you cover in the book.

Thank you.

Shakespeare has Henry V say to his troops, "All things are ready if our minds be so." Same goes for the intentions that will provide a focus as you lead change. Here are ways to develop the skills you need to make those intentions a reality.

BUILDING THE SKILLS YOU NEED

As Pfeffer and Sutton suggest, it's the doing part of the knowing-doing gap that often gets lost. Most of the managers I have worked with are pretty skilled at seeing what needs to happen at various points in the life of a change, but they often have difficulty turning that knowledge into action.

TOOLKIT For a copy of the knowledge and skills worksheet, visit www.askaboutchange.com and search for **knowledge and skills worksheet**.

As you reviewed chapters 2 through 9, you may have noticed places where your knowledge was spot-on and you had skills to match and other places where you had the knowledge but lacked the skills. Or perhaps you felt you lacked both knowledge and skills. No matter. Wherever you are is where you are. That's where to begin.

You might take this quick assessment, which corresponds with the content in chapters 2 through 9.

Score each on a 1 to 5 scale. 1 = No knowledge or skill, 2 = A tiny bit of knowledge or skill, 3 = Some knowledge and skill, 4 = A lot of knowledge and skill, 5 = Close to mastery

Topic	Knowledge	Skills
Cycle of Change		
Why people support and resist change		
Avoiding knee-jerk reactions		
Knowing the context		
Making a compelling case for change		
Getting started on the right foot		
Keeping change alive		
Getting back on track		

How do you develop skills? Don't go to training. Most management training can be great at providing knowledge, including knowledge about yourself through 360 surveys and psychological profiles and knowledge of concepts through lecture and exercises, but it often doesn't provide disciplined practice. And practice is what you need in order to get better.

Deliberate Practice

Geoff Colvin, in *Talent Is Overrated,* writes, "The factor that seems to explain the most about great performance is something researchers call deliberate practice. Exactly what that is and isn't turns out to be extremely important. It definitely isn't what most of us do on the job every day, which begins to explain the great mystery of the workplace—why we're surrounded by so many people who have worked hard for decades but have never approached greatness. Deliberate practice is also not what most of us do when we think we are practicing golf or the oboe or any other interests. Deliberate practice is hard. It hurts. But it works. More of it equals better performance. Tons of it equals great performance."[4]

People who have developed any degree of mastery in any field know that Colvin understands them. Great golfers spend countless hours trying to perfect various aspects of their game: they work on their drive, their putting game, getting out of a rough. Playing rounds of golf is usually not a significant part of their practice. Great pianists might prefer to sit down at a piano every morning and play through some Bach preludes and then move on to the Beethoven sonatas. While they do practice those pieces, they have spent untold hours working on developing their technique. Black belts in martial arts continue to work on moves and routines they learned when they were mere white belts.

At the end of an Aikido class, the teacher asked everyone to sit on the floor around him. He reminded us that we had spent most of the evening practicing just one martial arts move. He asked, "Do you want to know what the difference between a black belt and a white belt is?" Of course we did. He said that when we walked out of the warehouse that night into the dark parking lot, the white belts would do great if an attacker came at them in precisely the same way we had practiced for the past two hours. In other words, if the mugger not only came from behind but grabbed their left arm just below the elbow. But if the attacker came at them in another way, say from the right side or from a different angle, they would be lost. The black belts, on the other hand, would be able to adapt if that attack came from a different direction. That agility to learn a basic technique and then naturally adapt it to changing circumstances only comes from deliberate practice.

You can't go to a dojo three times a week, bow to a master instructor, and practice the skills of becoming a leader of change, but here is what you can do.

Practice IAG (Identify—Analyze—Generalize)

When I was first learning how to work with groups and organizations, I was studying at MATC, a Washington, D.C.–based organization that taught such things. After almost two years of immersion into their approach (with lots of time for practice), I went to an advanced workshop. We took turns facilitating the group for a couple of hours each and then got feedback. My turn came and I froze. Except for saying, "Hi, my name is Rick, and I'll be working with you for the next two hours," none of my interventions worked. They died. People either shrugged them off or ignored them.

At the end of the session, I asked the master trainer, John Denham, for feedback. He suggested that I come back at the end of the day when we could spend time together. I thought sure he was going to suggest that I consider leaving this profession and taking up taxidermy or some other pursuit that didn't require interaction with actual humans.

We talked for a few minutes and then he turned on the video that had been made during my session. He asked me to stop the video whenever I saw a place where it seemed like a good idea to intervene. When I stopped the tape, he asked what I had noticed. He asked what my intent was in intervening, and then he would play "the group" and I would intervene. Sometimes he responded in the way that I hoped he would, but at other times he took me down a rabbit hole. Then we would dissect what had just happened. By the end of a couple of hours, I felt great about my skills of observation and saying potentially useful things to a group. I had the knowledge, but something got in the way of doing. I had given in to knee-jerks. My need to perform in front of teachers and peers trumped my need to learn. John's patient debrief allowed me to get over my fear of intervening with such an august group of people in the room.

We used the IAG process for these debriefs. It is as simple as it is elegant. But for it to be effective, it demands rigorous and detached attention to what just happened. "Detached" in that you take all of the emotional and personal—I'm just no good—judgments out of the comments.

I = Identify. You identify the specific incident. The more specific you are, the better. If you can get it down to "Sean said X and I responded with Y," you have more to work with than trying to debrief an entire meeting. Remember, you are using this process to develop your skills. Once you try to debrief an entire three-hour meeting, you start to speak more generally. That type of debrief has its place, of course, but start with laser-like precision of a specific incident.

A = Analyze. Without judgment, examine what happened. "Sean said X." Note when he said it. His tone of voice. The context surrounding his comment. "I replied with Y." Look at your own tone of voice, etc. And then identify what happened next. Treat this the way court reporters do when they type what they are hearing without embellishment or commentary. This isn't a short story, but a transcript of what went on and what happened as a consequence of what was said or done.

G = Generalize. Here is a chance to learn from the experience. You could identify

- what you could do if something like this occurs again.
- what your options were in the incident with Sean.
- how what you just learned could help you in different types of situations.

IAG is quite simple. It might take a few minutes to go through the three steps, or you might spend an hour on it.

A good batter doesn't spend fifteen minutes in a batting cage and then step back and debrief the entire experience. He's probably going to Analyze what happened after every swing.

Action Learning

When Reginald (Reg) Revans (1907–2003) was a graduate student in astrophysics, he got a placement at the famed Cavendish Lab at Cambridge University. The lab had many world-renowned scientists, including five Nobel Laureates, and these very bright people shared ideas over tea once a week in a very collegial manner. This amazed him. His experience had taught him that there was a lot of ego in prestigious labs and that the scientists usually tried to put others down in order to reinforce their own brilliance. And here they were sharing ideas. As he looked closer, he found that in order to bring up a topic at the weekly tea, you had to have a problem. You couldn't talk about your latest achievement. I heard Revans say that when a Nobel Prize winner says, "I've got a problem," egos melt away as people try to help their esteemed colleagues.

Learning is as important as getting the project completed. He created an approach called Action Learning in which groups of people pull together to work on a project and learn while they are doing it. Learning happens as they work, it is not something that just happens at the end of the project. So imagine that these people are trying to learn teamwork. Not only would they work as a team, but they would stop periodically to reflect on what was occurring and what they were learning. IAG would be a good way to structure such a reflection period.

It helps if the project is one that is important but doesn't have a tight deadline. Otherwise, the looming deadline will trump learning and all the time will be spent on getting the task accomplished.

Experiments

Gestalt psychology teaches that experiments are a great way to learn. These are not exercises or planned events, but experiments that are created on the spot to help you learn something more about yourself and perhaps your behavior. For example, let's say you have a difficult time influencing your boss. When he begins to go all Alpha male on you, it triggers a knee-jerk reaction in you, and you respond by bringing out your Alpha male or female. You become like two baboons vying over a choice hunk of food.

You have a meeting scheduled for today at 10 and you kinda think that he will trigger you again. So you create an experiment. Here's what to do:

1. Make it a safe emergency. Whatever you plan to do, you need to feel that it is safe enough to try it, but risky enough so that you can learn from it. You devise an experiment in which you will remain absolutely silent whenever baboon-man triggers your desire to meet force with force. When you do speak, it will be to the topic of the meeting and not to his provocation. That's it. You think you can probably do that experiment—that's the safety part. But you don't feel all that comfortable remaining silent—that's the emergency. You promise yourself that you will do this at least once in the meeting.
2. You try the experiment. Your boss says something that triggers you. And you can feel your muscles begin to tense. Instead of speaking, you try to remain silent. That's all there is to it.
3. When the meeting is over, you think about what just happened using the Identify—Analyze—Generalize process.

Experiments can be a great way to try out new behaviors with relative safety. Perhaps you make the screen go blank on your PowerPoint just after the fifth slide. You step forward and ask the audience, "So, what do you think?" and then shut up until someone responds. For some people, that alone would be on the edge of their feeling of comfort. For others, the experiment might be to ask the question and then remain silent until you hear from five people. As small as these events are, they are the building blocks of mastery.

Walter Gieseking, the great pianist, would have his students take a tiny phrase in a long piece of music that was giving them trouble. He would tell them to work it over and over again. Playing faster, slower, with different rhythms, and in different keys. When those students saw that configuration later in the piece or in another piece, they would own that phrase. Like the black belt Aikido students who knew their moves so well that they could instinctively apply them in a variety of settings.

GETTING THE SUPPORT YOU NEED TO PRACTICE DELIBERATELY

Many organizations encourage managers and executives to get coaches. These people can be a great guide as you reflect on what you are doing and learn from it. For others, you may pick a buddy to help you. Consultants often use "shadow consultants" who are invisible to the client but are there to support the consultant in looking at his own work. My friend Massimo and I have been doing that for each other for years. We know each other so well by now that one can call the other and ask for a quick drive-by coaching session as one of us is headed to a meeting. An Action Learning group can serve the same purpose. And for some, keeping a personal journal can help you build your skills. Practice is essential. Pick a way that works for you.

As I write this chapter, the Winter Olympics are underway. As much as I marvel at what I see, I imagine the grueling practice it took for those men and women to make it to such a prestigious game. Learning a skill is a discipline and it takes time. But I know it is worth it. Earlier this week, I worked with a new client who had the instincts—or correct mindset, in my view—to lead change well. I would make small comments about what she might pay attention to or something she might try differently. It was clear that she had given a lot of thought to leading change, and I felt like I was coaching an Olympian. She knew what to do with what I suggested. I could see her think through my suggestions, tweak them, and make them her own (and disregard those comments that didn't quite fit for her). Such is the stuff of mastery.

I wish you well.

Endnotes

Chapter 1

1. Scott Keller and Carolyn Aiken, *The Inconvenient Truth About Change* (New York: McKinsey & Company, 2008).
2. Jeffrey Pfeffer and Robert Sutton, *The Knowing-Doing Gap* (Boston: Harvard Business School Press, 2000). This compelling book is well worth your time.
3. Hans Henrik Jorgensen, Lawrence Owen, and Andreas Neus, *Making Change Work* (New York: IBM, 2008), 7.
4. www.gallup.com.

Chapter 2

1. I adapted the Cycle of Change, with permission, from the Cycle of Experience created at the Gestalt Institute of Cleveland to describe a natural process for change.
2. Personal conversation with Kathie as I prepared to write the first edition of this book in 1995.
3. Rick Maurer, *Beyond the Wall of Resistance* (Austin, Tex.: Bard Press, 1996), 121–123.
4. Theodor Seuss Geisel ("Dr. Seuss"), *Green Eggs and Ham* (New York: Beginner Books, 1960).
5. David P. Hanna, quoting Arthur Jones, in *Designing Organizations for High Performance* (Reading, Mass.: Addison Wesley, 1988), 36.
6. Barbara Tuchman, *The March of Folly* (New York: Ballantine Books, 1990), 6.
7. Cooke and Wilder, from Maurer, *Beyond the Wall of Resistance*, 34–35.
8. William Bridges, *Managing Transitions* (Philadelphia: Da Capo Press, 2009), 3.
9. Arnold Beisser, "The Paradoxical Theory of Change." Originally published in Joen Fagan and Irma Lee Shepherd's *Gestalt Therapy Now* (Palo Alto, Calif.: 1970). Currently available online: http://www.gestalt.org/arnie.htm.

Chapter 3

1. Alex Gibney, "Paradise Tossed; How a Chance to Save American Capitalism Was Sabotaged at Eastern," The Free Library, June 1, 1986, http://www.thefreelibrary.com/Paradise tossed; how a chance to save American capitalism was . . . -a04262001 (accessed March 10, 2010). This site includes a lengthy article on the history of Eastern Airlines under Lorenzo. It is worth reading.
2. Robert Wright, *The Moral Animal* (New York: Pantheon, 1994), 280.
3. This section on the three levels is adapted from my e-book, *Introduction to Change Without Migraines* (Arlington, Va.: Maurer & Associates, 2009).
4. Felix Grant, quoted in Ken Ringle, "Felix Grant, for the Love of Jazz," *The Washington Post*, November 12, 1989, G1.

5. Everett M. Rogers, *The Diffusion of Innovations*, 3rd ed. (New York: Free Press, 1983), 32. Reprinted with permission of the publisher.
6. *New Grolier Multimedia Encyclopedia*, CD-ROM (Grolier Inc., 1993).
7. David Kenney, "Quality Standards That Can Destroy Quality," *Wall Street Journal*, November 11, 1993.

Chapter 4

1. Daniel Goleman, *Emotional Intelligence* (New York: Bantam, 2006).
2. Ted Conover, *New Jack* (New York: Vintage Books, 2001), 242–244.
3. Text excerpt from *Duck Soup*, used by permission. © Copyright Universal City Studios, Inc. Courtesy of MCA Publishing Rights, a Division of MCA, Inc. All rights reserved.
4. William Glaberson, "Week in Review," *New York Times*, October 9, 1994.
5. *Columbia Encyclopedia*, 5th ed., 1993.
6. Robert B. Cialdini, *Influence* (New York: Quill, 1984), 254–255. Before this fiasco, *Patton*, the highest-priced rental, went for $1.3 million less than *The Poseidon Adventure*, for a single showing on network television.

Chapter 5

1. Columbia Accident Investigation Board, 2003. <http://caib.nasa.gov/news/report/pdf/vol1/full/caib_report_volume1.pdf>.
2. Daniel J. Simons and Christopher F. Chabris, "Gorillas in Our Midst: Sustained Inattentional Blindness for Dynamic Events," *Perception* 28 (1999), 1063, citing an experiment by Neisser.
3. Douglas McGregor, *The Human Side of Enterprise* (New York: McGraw-Hill, 1960), 33.
4. Ibid., 33–44.
5. Ibid., 45–57.
6. Robert B. Cialdini, *Influence* (New York: Quill, 1984), 133.
7. Daryl Conner, *Managing at the Speed of Change* (New York: Villard Books, 1992).
8. Carol S. Dweck, *Mindset* (New York: Ballantine Books, 2006), 215.
9. Ibid., 15.
10. Ibid., 109.
11. Mindsets don't speak directly to making the morally right decisions, although a growth mindset is far less susceptible to hubris.
12. Jim Collins, *Good to Great* (New York: HarperCollins, 2001).
13. Dweck, *Mindset*, 110.
14. Ibid., 119.
15. Robert Wood and Albert Bandura, "Impact on Conceptions of Ability on Self-Regulatory Mechanisms and Complex Decision Making," *Journal of Personality and Social Psychology* 56 (1989), 407–415, as cited in Dweck, *Mindset*, 111.
16. Sterling Livingston,"Pygmalion in Management," *Harvard Business Review* (1969), 1.
17. Ibid., 2.
18. Ibid., 2.

Chapter 6

1. Scott Keller and Carolyn Aiken, *The Inconvenient Truth About Change* (New York: McKinsey & Company, 2008), 5.
2. Interview in 1991 with Nancy Badore, head of Ford's executive development process, for my first book, *Caught in the Middle* (Portland, Ore.: Productivity Press, 1992). Also, Badore's speech at the 1990 Organization Development Network conference.

3. Thomas J. Peters and Robert H. Waterman, *In Search of Excellence* (New York: Harper & Row, 1982).

Chapter 7

1. Large systems change is sometimes referred to as large group methods, whole systems change, and the list goes on.
2. Edwin A. Locke and Gary P. Latham, *Goal Setting: A Motivation Technique That Works!* (New York: Prentice Hall, 1984).
3. My interview with Barry Johnson in *The Gestalt Review* 6, no. 3 (2002), 210.
4. Interview with Marshall Orr, consultant in Richmond, Va., who has used this approach extensively, January 1995.
5. Interview with Kathie Dannemiller, April 2, 1995, in *Beyond the Wall of Resistance* (Austin, Tex.: Bard Press, 1996), 121–122.
6. Ibid., 122.

Chapter 8

1. Miles Cook, *Pulling Away and Sustaining Change* (Boston: Bain & Company, 2009), 3.
2. Michael Hammer and James Champy, *Reengineering the Corporation* (New York: Harper Business, 1993).
3. Ori Brafman and Rom Brafman, *Sway* (New York: Doubleday, 2008), 135.
4. The "Contract with Other Leaders" is adapted from my e-book, *Leading from the Middle* (Arlington, Va.: Maurer & Associates, 2008).
5. Jim Collins, *Good to Great* (New York: HarperCollins, 2001), 11.
6. Atul Gawande, *The Checklist Manifesto* (New York: Metropolitan Books, 2009).

Chapter 9

1. Ann Devroy, "U.S., Russia Sign Variety of Pacts as Talks Focus on Economics," *Washington Post*, September 29, 1994, A25.
2. Noel Tichy and Sherman Stratford, *Control Your Destiny or Someone Else Will* (New York: Doubleday, 1993), 244–246. Used by permission of the publisher.

Chapter 11

1. Yes, they were influenced by John Kotter's thinking on change. Forming a guiding coalition is one of the eight steps he identifies in *Leading Change* (Boston: Harvard Business School, 1995).
2. Robert Kegan and Lisa Lahey, *Immunity to Change* (Boston: Harvard Business School, 2009).
3. Ibid., 224.
4. Geoff Colvin, *Talent Is Overrated* (New York: Portfolio, 2008), 7.

Resources

www.askaboutchange.com

Throughout the book you've seen icons that look like this. 

I decided to put all the resources on a dedicated website. In that way, I can update resources and add new items easily.

In addition to the articles, podcasts, and assessments that you see referenced in the book, the website also includes a reading list. It is not an exhaustive list of every book published in the field of change. Rather, it is a list of books and articles that have influenced my thinking on change in organizations.

The site also includes a link to a free online community called the Change Management Open Source Project (www.changeOSP.com). There you'll meet people from around the world who are interested in leading change in organizations. The site also includes podcast interviews with experts in the field, some short homemade videos, an e-book titled *Introduction to Change Without Migraines*, and an active discussion forum fueled by your questions, responses, and opinions. I hope you'll consider joining us.

Toolkit Index

32 Free Online Resources

Page 78 scenario planning
A podcast with a brief introduction to scenario planning

Page 89 conditions for change
An assessment to help you spot what is working in your favor and where you need work to create the right conditions for change

Page 90 open book
A podcast and an article with a brief description of Open Book Management

Page 91 why before how
A podcast covering the most neglected point in the life of a change

Page 108 large systems change
Short written descriptions of some of the more popular approaches

Page 108 virtual change
Thoughts on large systems change in a virtual world

Page 112 create a vision
An article on how to create a vision statement

Page 114 Six Hats
A podcast introduction to de Bono's important Six Hats decision-making model

Page 118 support change questionnaire
An assessment to examine the extent to which your organization is likely to support any change you introduce

Page 127 change alive checklist
A list of things to remember in order to keep change alive

Page 133 contract with other leaders
A copy of this contract that you can reprint

Page 135 AAR discussion tool
Steps to include in an After Action Report

Page 137 23 ideas
An article in which people in the field share what has worked for them to keep change alive

Page 139 sustain change
A podcast interview with J. R. McGee on ways to sustain commitment to change

Index

Acknowledgments

I wish I could list all of my clients by name. I have learned so much about why people support and why they resist change from you. You demanded that I be clear. Get rid of jargon. And most of all, be practical. My work is better for having had the privilege to work with you.

Thanks to Herb Stevenson and Rick Seikaly, buddies and colleagues, who read the section on context and gave their suggestions and critique. Since that chapter is so central to this book, their influence can be felt well beyond that single chapter. Thanks to all the fine people at Bard Press: Ray Bard, Sherry Sprague, Deborah Costenbader, Luke Torn, Joe Pruss, Randy Miyake and Patti Zeman at Hespenheide Design, Kay Banning, and Leslie Stephen, who is a truly fine editor and just plain fun to work with. Thanks to all of you who allowed me to include interviews with you in this book. Thanks to the many corporate leaders I interviewed for this book. I'll keep my promise and not mention you by name. The enthusiasm, support, and wisdom from all these people kept this labor of love from turning into just raw labor. And thanks to members of the Change Management Open Source Project (www.changeOSP.com) who provided ideas and helpful critique. Same appreciation goes to a couple of discussion forums on LinkedIn.

When I wrote the first version of this book, I had been studying at the Gestalt Institute of Cleveland for a few years. Since 1996 I have taught there five to six weeks a year in programs geared to people who lead and consult in organizations. The faculty and students in Cleveland continue to provide a model of intellectual rigor and good practice. And I would not have thought to write this book, nor could I have, without the profound influence and support I received from the faculty and fellow participants in the first major program I attended in Cleveland from 1991–1993.

A special thanks to Jeffrey Pfeffer and Robert Sutton, authors of *The Knowing-Doing Gap*, and Robert Kegan and Lisa Laskow Lahey, authors of

Immunity to Change. They graciously allowed me to use their thinking and frameworks in this book.

And here are the acknowledgments from the first edition. My admiration for what these people provided still stands.

Thanks to Matt Kayhoe and Max Stark, two fellow consultants who have influenced my thinking in many ways, from out-and-out, but always friendly, criticism of my ideas to lengthy explorations of the subject with me. Others whose ideas have helped me learn more about resistance are Phil Kalin, Maureen Keamey, Eleanor Hooks, Brenda Jones, Diane Johnson, Michael Matthews, Dinah Nieburg, Susan Schroeer, Neil Sklarew, and Jim Vanderbeck. Thanks to Warren Conner, a fine instructor of T'ai Chi and willing recipient of all manner of questions on the relationship of martial arts to organizational life.

In addition to many already named, I am grateful to those who read early drafts or portions of the manuscript and made helpful comments: Chip Bell, Geoff Bellman, Sam Grouse, Carol Dana, Margo Freehurg, Larry Knox, John Mariotti, Tom Martinec, Kathi Mocniak, Kathy Monte, LeRoy Pingho, Diane Porterfield, Kay Scott, Michael C. Thomas, Sherry Weinstein, and Marc Young. A special note of thanks to clients, leaders of organizations, and colleagues who met with me to talk about what they wanted to see in a book like this.

Thanks to the people who granted interviews. In most cases I was able to use only a small portion of what I gained from them, but I appreciate the fullness of their generosity.

Thanks to Jodi Sleeper-Triplet, who was my business manager back then, who protected my time and ran the business so that I could actually write this book. Thanks to my wife, Kathy, who prodded me often with the question, "So, are you ever going to write this book?" And for her encouragement throughout the process. Words can hardly express my appreciation for her constant support.

About the Author

Frasierphoto.com

Rick Maurer is an advisor to leaders in large organizations on ways to plan and implement change successfully—in other words, apply the ideas he covers in this book.

Many organizations and consulting firms have applied Rick's unique approach to leading change, including *The Washington Post*, Lockheed Martin, Deloitte Consulting, American Management Systems, AARP, Tulane University Hospital and Clinic, Bell Atlantic (Verizon), FAA, Mount Sinai NYU Medical Center, Charles Schwab, Sandia National Labs, Urban Library Institute, National GeoSpatial Intelligence Agency, the District of Columbia Public Schools, the International Monetary Fund, and many other corporations, nonprofits, and federal and local agencies.

He started the popular Change Management Open Source Project, a free resource for people from around the world who are interested in leading change in organizations (www.changeOSP.com).

Since publication of the first edition of this book, Rick's opinion has been sought by *The Wall Street Journal, Fortune,* NBC Nightly News, CNBC, *The Washington Post, The New York Times, The Economist, USA Today, Industry Week, Fast Company,* and *Investor's Business Daily.*

In addition, Rick teaches at The Gestalt Institute of Cleveland. He is the author of several books on leadership and change, including *Why Don't You Want What I Want?* and the *Feedback Toolkit*. He is also a fledgling part-time jazz musician in the Washington, D.C. area.

You can contact him at 703-525-7074.

For more information about Rick's work, visit www.rickmaurer.com, www.changemanagementnews.com (blog), and www.askaboutchange.com (free resources for leading change).